on the cover:
Verdi, portrait by G. Boldini
Milan, "G. Verdi"
rest home for musicicans

on this page:
bust of Verdi
by Vincenzo Gomito
Milan, Museum of La Scala Theatre

Text by Gino Pugnetti

Translated from the Italian by Raymond Rosenthal

First published in Italian under the title I GRANDI DI TUTTI I TEMPI:
Verdi by Arnoldo Mondadori Editore S.p.A., Milan

First American Edition

published by

Elite Publishing Corporation
11-03 46th Avenue
Long Island City, New York 11101

Library of Congress Catalog Card Number: 84-48130
ISBN: 0-918367-00-X

Printed and bound in Italy by Officine Grafiche
Arnoldo Mondadori Editore, Verona, Italy, May 1984.

VERDI

ELITE PUBLISHING CORPORATION

VERDI'S MOTHER FLEES IN TERROR FROM THE RUSSIANS

On the evening of October 10, 1813, Carlo Verdi closed his store early and at eight o'clock that night, by candle-light, in the old house at Le Roncole sunk in mist, his first son Giuseppe was born. His birth certificate was written in French, for the Grand Duchy of Parma was under Napoleonic rule, and so little Verdi was called Joseph Fortunin François, the son of Carlo Verdi and Luigia Uttini.

Le Roncole was, as it is today, a small village a few miles from Busseto, just a handful of houses and good land. In Carlo Verdi's store were sold foodstuffs, salt, coffee, tobaccos, business deals were closed glass in hand, and wandering musicians would come in and play. Certainly their tavern songs were the first notes the little boy heard.

After the disaster at Beresina in 1812, out of Napoleon's 700,000 men 30,000 had returned from Russia in a pitiful state. And in 1813 all of Europe was ranged against Napoleon. During that same year the Emperor had sent his faithful Vice-Roy Eugene to Italy in an attempt to organize a defense. A squadron of Russian cavalry had pushed as far as Le Roncole and Verdi's mother, terrified, clasping the child in its swaddling clothes, had barely managed, together with the village's women, to find shelter in the bell-tower, thus avoiding being trampled to death by that rabble. In that same church, some years later, Giuseppe was to make his first conscious contact with music.

The country boy grew up serious and good-natured, solitary and shy. With the church only two steps away, he was often called to serve Mass. One Sunday he stood there as if entranced by the magical sound of the old organ and to rouse him from his dream the priest had to give him a shove. The altar boy tripped on his long tunic, banged his head on the altar steps and let slip a countryman's oath: "May God strike you with a lightning bolt!" A few years later, as if in an opera, the poor priest was actually struck down by lightning.

Convinced of his son's deep passion for music, Carlo Verdi bought him a broken-down spinet; the craftsman Stefano Cavaletti repaired it and inside he carved the words "... seeing young Giuseppe Verdi's desire for learning to play this instrument is enough for me to be completely satisfied. Year of the Lord, 1821." The date indicates that Verdi began to study the piano at the age of eight.

In the wake of the patriotic experience formed under French domination, in 1820-1822 there exploded in Italy a number of insurrections which the rulers of the Peninsula suppressed, resorting to much harsher police measures; also in the Duchy of Parma people had been sentenced to jail and exile. In this climate of yearning for freedom, Verdi's personality was formed. From left: Maria Luisa awards diplomas to the students at the National Academy of Fine Arts.
Ciro Menotti, one of the leaders of the Este conspiracy in 1831, sentenced to die by hanging by Francesco IV of Modena.

Busseto, a small village of a few thousand souls, has been the property of the ancient Pallavicino family which until the 17th century had favored the arts and scholarship. At the beginning of the 19th century, the cultural activities of the ciry were subsidized by the Monte di Pietà which also helped hospitals, libraries and schools.

Below: the exterior and living room of Antonio Barezzi's house in Busseto. It flaunted a certain luxury: decorated ceilings, carpets, a Viennese Fritz piano on which Verdi could play from time to time. Signora Barezzi, frightened by a crime which took place in the town, insisted that young Verdi also sleep in her house.

HIS FATHER WANTED HIM TO BECOME A COUNTRY BAND LEADER

Seeing that his son made good progress with his musical studies, Carlo Verdi was seized by the ambition to make him a band leader. So he decided that Giuseppe should receive his first lessons lfrom the village organist, Baistrocchi. The results were so felicitous that, when the old teacher left his post, none other than Verdi – then twelve years old – became Le Roncole's organist. The instrument was broken down, asthmatic, antiquated, but he was able to earn 100 lire a year with it, including his extracurricular services for weddings and christenings, which amounted to 30 to 40 thousand lire in today's money. His father, who as a good native of Parma was a music lover, realized that the boy should continue his studies. Making some sacrifices, he then sent him to Busseto which, for the people in Le Roncole, was something of a musical capital, entrusting him to a shoemaker friend named Pugnatta for room and board at 40 *centesimi* a day and to the priest Don Pietro Seletti for the study of Latin. Though living in Busseto, Giuseppe did not give up his post as village organist. On the dawn of every feast-day he walked the three miles that separated him from Le Roncole; one misty Sunday he slipped into a ditch out of which he was fished by a peasant who responded to his cries for help. During those very months his good star guided the boy on the path of his destiny. His father received his food-stuff supplies from a Busseto grocer, Antonio Barezzi. Through this business relationship Barezzi met the young Giuseppe, became interested in his studies, and when he saw his obvious musical talent he helped him, offering him a job as a clerk in his store. In the evening Barezzi – an amateur musician – gave Giuseppe lessons in wind instruments. He then introduced him to the director of Busseto's music school, Ferdinando Provesi, choir master and organist at the cathedral. This was also a fortunate encounter, since Provesi immediately saw young Verdi's talent, admitted him to the rehearsals of Busseto's Philarmonic, made him copy the orchestra parts, and gradually let him take his place on the Philarmonic's podium. Thus the boy was able to gain a deeper knowledge of the music of Haydn, Porpora, and Rossini. After having entered a competition for the post of organist in a nearby town, Soragna (he lost to a competitor with connections), Barezzi proposed that Verdi should continue his studies in Milan with a scholarship of 300 lire from the Monte di Pietà.

Left: the harpsichord on which Verdi practiced with Maestro Lavigna, and a small volume of Cicero's letters that Verdi studied. Below: the spinet given to Verdi as a gift by Barezzi; the music teacher Ferdinando Provesi; the Latin teacher Don Seletti. Only after hearing the boy play the organ did Seletti become convinced that Verdi should give up Latin for music.

Left: a portrait of Barezzi and the manuscript of a juvenile Tantum Ergo by Verdi who in his old age repudiated it with these words: "I advise the unhappy owner of this composition to throw it in the fire. These notes do not have the slightest value." Antonio Barezzi was born in Busseto in 1787 and was the oldest of three brothers, all passionate art lovers. From an alcohol distillery and a store specializing in colonial goods, Barezzi made a very comfortable living. This allowed him to act the Maecenas, holding musical evenings in his house and subsidizing public concerts.

FLUNKED AT HIS EXAM HE CANNOT ENTER CONSERVATORY

Accompanied by his father and Maestro Provesi, Verdi arrived in Milan by coach at the end of May, 1832. He was tall and thin with chestnut hair, an aquiline nose, a dark beard and some pock marks on his face. He felt out of place in the big city. He rented rooms on Via Santa Maria, in the house of the nephew of his teacher Don Seletti, and immediately submitted an application to be admitted as a paying student in the Royal Imperial Conservatory. He underwent the mandatory exam for admission, playing a piece on the piano and presenting some of his compositions. But eight days later, meeting Maestro Alessandro Rolla, the director of La Scala and a "big wheel" at the Conservatory, he learned the bitter truth: the commission had turned him down. Why? First of all, his status as a "foreigner" had been a negative factor. In fact, the Conservatory was tremendously overcrowded and students from Lombardy-Veneto region fought over the instruments in order to study. Besides, the maximum age of admission was fourteen and he was eighteen and a half. Finally, the commission had noted the faulty position of the young autodidact's hands, nor had it been impressed by his modest countryman's appearance. So,

flunked more for bureaucratic than technical reasons, the judges recognized that Verdi "could presumably succeed in composing." Maestro Rolla advised him to study privately with Vincenzo Lavigna, a native of Apulia, trained in the Neapolitan school and a protegee of Paisiello. And that's just what Verdi did. Like his predecessor, Maestro Lavigna also realized quite soon the talents the young man possessed, offered him his experience and friendship, took him into his house, and urged him to go to La Scala to explore the 18th century classics and immerse himself in Mozart and Beethoven.

In 1834 Lavigna took Verdi to the Teatro dei Filodrammatici to attend the rehearsals of Haydn's *Creation* conducted by Maestro Pietro Massimi. One evening the substitute fell sick and Verdi was kindly invited to take his place and continue the rehearsal. He sat down at the piano, playing with one hand and conducting with the other; the musicians in the orchestra followed him whit increasing enthusiasm, and so it was decided to entrust him with the execution of the oratorio. It was a remarkable success. *The Creation* was then repeated at the Casino dei Nobili before the Milanese aristocracy.

Facing page: the Galleria De Cristoforis and a view of Milan at the beginning of the 19th century. On the left: Francesco Basily, censor of the Conservatory; the composers Paer and Enrico Herz, whose pieces Verdi played at the piano exam.
Below: Piazza del Duomo by Inganni, and the Naviglio around 1840 (Milan Museum).

Verdi needed a passport to come to Milan because the Veneto Region and the Duchy of Milan (called the Lombard-Venetian Kingdom) were under the rule of the Emperor of Austria. In 1832, the year in which Verdi went to Milan, Silvio Pellico's book Le mie prigioni *was published. Milan, when Verdi saw it, did not have more than 150,000 inhabitants, but it was the most important center in Italy, also for theatrical activities. Cultural life was intense, singers were signed up in the cafés, and music publishers such as Ricordi, Lucca and Canti were making a name for themselves.*

HE MARRIES
THE DAUGHTER OF
HIS BENEFACTOR

Verdi was touched by the first deep sorrow of his life in 1832 when his sister Giuseppina, beautiful but mentally backward, died. The next year, more sad news: the death of Maestro Provesi. The Busseto Philarmonic was without a conductor and Verdi was called upon to replace his first and dearly loved teacher. But since the post also included the job of organist in the cathedral, a not very edifying series of events occurred in Busseto's life. The ecclesiastical authorities insisted on their own candidate for organist, a certain Ferrari from Guastalla, and the population split into two factions: the supporters of Verdi and those of Ferrari. There were scorching insults and satiric remarks from both sides, and even brawls. When the echo of the vehement conflict reached Parma, the government decided that the post should be awarded after a competitive exam. In 1835 the exam was held and the examiner – the court organist Giuseppe Alinovi – did not hesitate to give the victory to Verdi. Now with a secure post, Verdi married Margherita Barezzi, the daughter of his benefactor. Giuseppe and Maria knew each other since childhood, and while he was giving her piano lessons, they fell in love. Margherita was attractive, sweet, serene, full of admiration for her Giuseppe's musical gifts. They were married on May 4, 1936, with all the members of Busseto's Philarmonic in attendance. After a short trip to Milano they came back to town, where Papa Barezzi set them up in Palazzo Rusca, providing for all their needs. Verdi was happy, bursting with enthusiasm: there was not a feast-day that he did not take his players to perform somewhere in the province; he held study concerts at home and set about composing his first opera, *Oberto*. And a girl, was born, Virginia, for whom the young father composed a moving lullaby. But happy days were soon followed by months of sorrow: his old teacher, Lavigna, died unexpectedly in Milan; in 1838 a boy was born, Icilio, but a month later little Virginia died. Verdi withdrew into himself, deeply saddened, and he could no longer bear to live in Busseto. He resigned the posts that had gained him so much acclaim from the people of Busseto, and moved to Milan with his family. Accompanied by everyone's good wishes and also by the help of his father-in-law Barezzi, he found hospitality with Seletti, who had welcomed him during his first stay in Milan.

In oval: Margherita Barezzi in a painting by A. Mussini.
Below: Verdi, during the first years of his stay in Milan, and, next to him, the impresario Bartolomeo Merelli. A youthful error had forced Merelli to interrupt his law studies and get a job with a theatrical agency. He directed theaters in St. Petersburg, Paris, London, and Berlin but La

Scala was his general headquarters. He was called the "Napoleon of impresarios". He lived lavishly; he died suddenly in Milan on April 10, 1879.
Further below: Gaisruck, the Archbishop of Milan, crowns Ferdinand of Austria in the city's Duomo; the Corsia dei Servi in 1836 in a painting by G. Canella in the Museum of Milan.

Verdi experienced grave difficulties in Milan, so much so that he was down to a single meal a day, which he took in a modest tavern. Below, two Milanese taverns, well known in the 19th century: the Osteria della Cazzoeula and (below that) the Osteria della Cassina di Pomm. The first, towards Linate, was the setting in 1733 for an amorous adventure of Goldoni's.

But it was also a meeting place in 1848 of a small group of patriots to which belonged Amatore Sciesa called Antonio, who uttered the famous "tirem innanz" (forge on). The Cassina di Pomm had many illustrious customers, among whom could be numbered Casanova and Stendhal. Porta also wrote a poem about it.

OBERTO, HIS FIRST OPERA STAGED AT LA SCALA

In Milan Verdi had met one of the most famous prima donnas of the period, the soprano Giuseppina Strepponi and, on the piano, he had played for her the score of his first opera. *Oberto, Conte di San Bonifacio*. Having obtained her favorable opinion, convincing the impresario Bartolomeo Merelli – Strepponi's friend – to accept the opera for La Scala was rather easy. At last Verdi was about to achieve his dream. But at the rehearsals the tenor Napoleone Moriani fell sick: the performance had to be postponed, indeed actually cancelled. Verdi was in despair and determined to return to Busseto. But one morning Merelli sent a messenger for him from La Scala, welcomed him cordially, told him that he had been favorably impressed by *Oberto*'s rehearsals and offered him a contract: the impresario would pay the costs of staging the opera, and the receipts would be divided between him and Verdi. Verdi accepted the conditions, rented a house on Via Simone at Porta Ticinese, so as to work calmly in the quiet of his family. Here, on October 12, 1839, a year and a half after his sister, little Icilio also passed away. Though he was in great despair Verdi still had to immerse himself in work because all his hopes rested in *Oberto*. And the opera was performed at La Scala on November 17, 1839. He was highly excited. Between the first and second acts he ran home to tell the good news to Margherita who had remained alone and in suspense: the audience was applauding, the opera was actually going to be a success. Satisfied, Merelli offered Verdi new librettos in order to continue their collaboration. The maestro chose the least objectionable, *Il finto Stanislao*, taken from a French farce. Indeed, Merelli wanted a comic opera. Verdi's two children had just died, and it is easy to imagine in what mood he set about composing this light-hearted music. Then for Verdi the terrible year of 1840 began. He fell sick; he found himself in financial difficulties. On June 18, 1840 Margherita also passed away, a victim of encephalitis. Desperate, Verdi fled to Busseto, torn by grief and sorrow. But Merelli was the impresario and reminded him of his commitment. Verdi was forced to return to Milan and complete the comic opera, *Un giorno di Regno* (this is the title given to *Il finto Stanislao*) which failed to the tune of indifference and boos at La Scala.

To the left: frontispiece of the libretto of Oberto preserved at La Scala's Theatrical Museum. The opera showed traces of the influence of Bellini and Donizetti, nevertheless the publisher Giovanni Ricordi saw Verdi's originality and bought Oberto for 1,750 francs. This was the beginning of the bond between Verdi and the Ricordi Publishing House, which will continue all the way to Falstaff. Further left: label of a liqueur named after the Monza tram, a typical element of the life of the time. Above: Piazza della Scala, as it looked at the time of Oberto (a canvas by Inganni).

HE ATE ONLY
A MEAL A DAY
NEVERTHELESS
NABUCCO IS BORN

After the destruction of his family and the collapse of his artistic hopes, Verdi continued to live in Milan. Sad, taciturn, and so poor that he could permit himself only one meal a day in a tavern on Via Durini. At the end of that tragic year 1840, on a night of snow, just as he came out of the De Cristoforis Galleria, the young maestro bumped into Merelli. The impresario – who still believed in him – linked his arm in his and, amiably, first told him of his troubles at the opera, then he said that the composer Aldo Nicolai had rejected a libretto entitled *Nabucodonosor* and he was looking for another libretto to give him instead. Verdi proposed *Il Proscritto*, which Merelli had received earlier, and together they went to search for it in La Scala's archives. Taking advantage of the situation, Merelli asked Verdi to do him the favor of reading the *Nabucodonosor* libretto that Nicolai had turned down, and shoved it into his coat pocket. Having gotten home, the maestro threw the libretto, which was written in large script, on the table, and it opened to the verses *"Va pensiero, sull'ali dorate"*. Verdi was struck by these words. He went to bed but was unable to fall asleep. He lit the lamp and read the libretto three times over. But in the morning – still stubborn – he took the manuscript back to Merelli who – even more stubborn – rammed it back into his pock-

et, shoving him out the door. Verdi, who was just overcoming a terrible crisis, tried to compose. The notes came slowly, with difficulty, then, miraculously, faster and faster as Verdi was gripped by a creative frenzy. Thus was born *Nabucco*, the opera which would lay the foundations for his future glory. The opera was completed in October, 1841. It opened at La Scala on March 9, 1842, staged on the cheap, with scenery and costumes out of the warehouse. But already during rehearsals stage hands and lighting men left their work to listen to this new music, this new style. It was the premonitory sign of the success to follow. When the opera was performed, the maestro, as was the custom then, listened to it seated in the orchestra. And the audience sensed immediately the new Verdian vein, a masculine art, unusual, essential. They often interrupted the performance with bouts of frenetic applause, and the chorus *"Va pensiero"* had to be repeated. In the end, an immense ovation burst out for the maestro who bowed, pallid, without a smile. Among the famous spectators that evening was Gaetano Donizetti and, among those from Busseto, Giovanni, poor Margherita's brother, who had come to Milan with a purse of gold coins to gain the favor of the claque. Certainly, there was no need for that.

On opposite page: costumes for Nabucco: *Baldassarre and Abigaille, preserved at La Scala Museum, and the piano score.* Below: Giuseppina Strepponi, *famous soprano, first interpreter of* Nabucco. *It was rumored that she had had a relationship with the impresario Merelli. During the* Nabucco *period, the soprano became intimate with Verdi.*

Below: *the interior of La Scala around 1830. Further down: Verdi and Bellini at the time of their successes. Like* Nabucco, Norma, *with its impassioned choruses, aroused the nationalism of the spectators. In those years the Italian political climate had been maturing. Culture was spreading and the theaters became the*

meeting place of poets and patriots. In the Jews' drama in Nabucco *the audience saw the anguish of the oppressed Italians, and so the opera was also regarded as a political success. Verdi became a fashionable composer: hats and ties were made named after him and even various dishes "a la Verdi" were created.*

For the opera to follow Nabucco *Merelli did not fill in the figure on the contract. Strepponi advised Verdi to ask for 8,000 Austrian lire, as much as Bellini had received for* Norma. *The new opera was* I Lombardi *(1843) which was followed by* Ernani *(1844),* I due Foscari *(1844),* Giovanna d'Arco *(1845) and* Attila *(1846).*

In 1847 there was Macbeth, *Verdi's first encounter with Shakespeare; the opera was staged at La Pergola in Florence.* Macbeth *was only partly understood and received an unfavorable opinion also from the poet Giuseppe Giusti.*
Here below: the frontispieces of I Lombardi *and* Macbeth, *and a modern stage setting for* Ernani *(La Scala theater).*

TRIUMPH IS REPEATED WITH I LOMBARDI AND THEN WITH ERNANI

Verdi was saved. While La Scala successfully continued the performances of *Nabucco*, he was already thinking of his new opera, *I Lombardi alla prima Crociata*. The music was ready in six months, but the censorship objected to the libretto. The Austrian archbishop of Milan, Gaisruck, informed that processions, baptisms, and the Valley of Jehoshaphat figured in the story, asked the authorities to forbid its performance. Verdi, Merelli, and the librettist Solera were summoned by the chief of police, the Italian Torresani, but Verdi refused to go. The skillful Merelli convinced the functionary to authorize the performance, promising to substitute "Ave Maria" with "Salve Maria". The opera could therefore be staged at La Scala on February 11, 1843. The episode of the conflict with the censorship became well known and even magnified greatly and already by afternoon the entrances to the theater and the streets nearby were packed with people. The success of *I Lombardi* was similar to that of *Nabucco*. This time too the height of enthusiasm was aroused by a chorus. "O Signore, dal tetto natio" (O Lord, from our native land). The nostalgia of the Lombards on crusade became identified with the national aspirations of the spectators, who awarded the composer an incredible triumph.

In the wake of these emotional successes, Count Carlo Mocenigo, director of La Fenice Theater in Venice, commissioned a new opera for the 1843-44 season. As a subject he suggested Victor Hugo's *Ernani*, which was all the rage in France; as librettist he recommended a young literary man from Murano, Francesco Maria Piave. Verdi accepted. This time too the censorship objected to the book because it put on stage a plot against an emperor, but the change of a few verses was enough to obtain the go-ahead. Despite the mediocrity of the singers, on March 9, 1844, the Venetians received *Ernani* with great warmth. The third chorus "Si ridesti il leon di Castiglia" (Awaken, lion of Castille) unleashed the patriotism of the spectators, who saw their lion of San Marco in that image. At the fourth repeat performance the enthusiasm burst out so impetuously that Verdi was carried on the Venetians' shoulders into Piazza San Marco. With this opera, Verdi's youthful inspiration ended; new commitments awaited him in the theaters of the world.

Here at left: pictures of Milan in the early 19th century: the portico of Sant'Ambrogio, and the interior of the church during a ceremony: one can see the Austrian soldiers who inspired Giusti with one of his most famous anti-Hapsburg poems.
In the two portraits: Verdi at the time of I due Foscari *and Gaetano Ferri, the famous baritone from Parma, in* Ernani.

17

1848: VERDI IS NOW THE SYMBOL OF A FREE ITALY

It is 1848: all of Europe is in an upheaval, following the example of Paris which, having overturned the government of Louis Phillipe, proclaimed a republic. Vienna and Berlin rise up (Wagner will also be on the barricades) and in Italy the first agitations flare up with, in January, uprisings in Messina and Palermo. These were followed by preoccupying demonstrations in Naples, where Ferdinand II was forced to liberalize the constitution, soon to be imitated by Leopold II of Tuscany, Carlo Alberto in Piedmont, and Pius IX. In the Lombardy-Veneto region the tumult reached its peak during the Five Days of Milan from March 18 to 22. This is a glorious page in the history of the nation: the insurgents fought from roofs and windows, and shot even from the spires of the Duomo until in desperation Radetzky's troops were forced to withdraw from the city. At the dawn of March 23, 1848, the banner of liberty flew over Milan; Parma and Modena also drove out their oppressors. Later on, the defeat of Custoza at the hands of the Austrian armies returned the sovereigns to their thrones.

After the military overturns, the struggle in Italy continued, hidden, inexorable, obstinate, and Verdi who in the previous years had become the musical symbol of a free Italy, thought of an opera whose notes could kindle even more the faith of the Italians. After rejecting a story about Cola di Rienzo, the maestro's attention was attracted by the battle of Legnano, the first Italian victory over a German emperor. He felt he would be able to set it to music with spontaneous emotion and it would be received with enthusiasm. And so it was. *La Battaglia di Legnano* was staged in Rome at the Argentina Theater on January 27, 1849. Already during rehearsals masses of people managed to get into the theater to acclaim Verdi. At the premiere there was not a single empty seat nor a libretto to be bought: the audience in the theater flaunted flags, pennants and cocades, acclaiming Verdi and Italy together, insisting by their cheers that the entire fourth act be repeated. It was a political success. After the defeat of Novara in 1849, Carlo Alberto had abdicated in favor of his son Vittorio Emanuele II; the Roman Republic tried in vain to hold out against the French who entered Rome on July 3, 1849, and returned the Pope to power. Brief, therefore, was the enthusiasm aroused by *La battaglia di Legnano*.

In 1849 Verdi, on Giuseppe Mazzini's request, set a patriotic hymn to the verses of the young Genoese poet Goffredo Mameli, who later died in the defense of the Roman Republic. But the composition did not obtain the vast popularity of the Hymn of Mameli composed by Michele Novaro, which opens with the words Fratelli d'Italia, today the anthem of the Italian Republic. In the prints to the left, some images of the Five Days of Milan (1848). On the left below: fighting at Porta Romana, barricades on Piazza di San Calimero. The area of Baggio after the revolution, and the Corsia del Giardino. In the large painting: the battle of Porta Tosa, from behind the barricades.

IN LONDON THE QUEEN ATTENDS THE PREMIERE OF I MASNADIERI

The first European capitals to welcome and acclaim Giuseppe Verdi were London and Paris. In July, 1847, the maestro went to London to conduct the new opera *I Masnadieri* at the Queen's Theater, also called Theater of the Italians, where the superintendent was the intelligent impresario Lumley. On the night of the premiere of *I Masnadieri* there was a sumptuous reception: Queen Victoria and almost the entire English parliament attended. The opera was a success, the receipts for the repeat performances very high, and impresario Lumley was tempted to offer Verdi the directorship of the Theater of the Italians, which together with Covent Garden enjoyed great prestige for the quality of the Italian repertory it presented. Besides, Lumley asked Verdi to commit himself to composing a new opera each year, for three consecutive years. Verdi declared himself willing to accept if given 60,000 lire a year for the new opera, 30,000 lire for the post of director, a house in the country, and a carriage. Lumley agreed. However, organizational difficulties wrecked the project. Verdi would glady have lived in London. It was a city he liked a great deal. But he had some reservations about the climate and wrote to his friend Countess Maffei: "With this constant smell of coal I feel I am always aboard a steamship". But the great city fascinated him so much that he declared that if it had had the sky of Naples there would be no point in searching for paradise. His friend Giuseppina Strepponi also loved England and wanted to gain a deeper knowledge of the English soul. So she studied the language and learned it well enough to read and write it correctly. As a result Strepponi was able to take care of Verdi's correspondence in his business relations with Great Britain. To this day the English continue to return Verdi's friendship, proving to be convinced lovers of opera, especially Verdi's operas.

Im his way, Verdi also loved Paris, where he lived for years and returned many times. Giuseppina Strepponi, when still young, realized that her voice was failing and decided to teach singing in Paris, the capital of the arts and, from 1847 on, Verdi began visiting her frequently. They esteemed and loved each other and decided to live together. In 1848 they had an apartment on Rue de la Victoire 18 bis, but they had also rented a villa in the country, at Passy, where they spent quiet days of heppiness. So Verdi stayed gladly in Paris, not only because of its Opera, but also because he felt anonymous there and did not have to account to anyone for his irregular relationship with Giuseppina.

The Tuileries, the royal residence built in Paris at the behest of Catherine de' Medici, was a favorite stop on Verdi's strolls (in the painting at left: Dinner at the Tuileries by C. Baron). Here below: the poster of a large Paris store. Wherever they went Verdi and Strepponi liked to shop: everything, from clothes to furniture and knick-knacks. In Paris, Verdi also bought a piano. Below: Gioacchino Rossini in a caricature by Carjat. The relations between Verdi and Rossini were always characterized by humorous sallies. The salutation in a letter written by Rossini to Verdi reads: "Rossini, ex-composer and pianist of the fourth rank, to the illustrious composer Verdi, pianist of the fifth rank." In the two pictures on the right: the Italian Theater at Paris around 1830 and a London street in the middle of the 19th century. In London Verdi met several times with Giuseppe Mazzini and one evening, at Lumley's, he had dinner with the exiled Louis Bonaparte.

SCANDAL AT BUSSETO OVER THE RELATIONSHIP WITH STREPPONI

At the beginning of August, 1849, Verdi and Strepponi, having left Paris where a cholera epidemic had broken out, returned to Busseto to live in Palazzo Orlandi, which Verdi had bought. In that patrician dwelling the maestro began to work with a certain tranquillity on the score of *Luisa Miller*, while waiting to move to the villa at Sant'Agata, where the first of his masterpieces, *Rigoletto*, was born. The people in Busseto, in those years, were already at loggerheads with their Verdi. The animosity had begun in 1845, when the maestro denied ever having promised his interest and influence to bring two famous singers to the summer opera season at Busseto. This misunderstanding was just the prelude. Verdi's reserved and aloof life, which the people in Busseto would have liked to be more cordial and closer to them, aroused resentment in many. A salient episode, which brought into focus the faults on both sides occurred years later, in 1859, when the construction of a new theater was started in Busseto and Verdi objected to the expense, which he regarded as illogical at such a difficult moment for the Italian economy. Despite his attitude, the theater was built (but only in 1868) and the people in Busseto hoped that the composer would write a new opera for its opening. Verdi didn't want to hear of it, also because of a quarrel with the mayor. However, convinced by his friend Dr. Carrara, he reluctantly agreed that the theater should at least bear his name. Only then did he subscribe the considerable sum of ten thousand lire for building expenses. Among the fundamental reasons for the hostile relationship with his fellow citizens, a strong influence was exerted by the unfriendly attitude of certain people who harshly criticized his tie with Strepponi. Anonymous letters sent to him from Busseto greatly embittered him. It was after having received one of these shameful missives that Verdi gave the box that had been assigned to him for life in the new theater to a friend, swearing that he would never set foot in it. On several occasions the people of Busseto threw it up to Verdi that they had given him money to study, but they got a sharp reply: "I have returned the money! The moral debt remains. But I can proudly say: I carried your name out into the world and that is well worth one thousand two hundred francs.!" And when the people of Busseto boasted: "We made Verdi!" he replied, "Try and make more of them!"

The main square in Busseto with the Rocca Pallavicino, from the name of the family which since the 17th century had promoted the arts in the town. To the left of the tower, Palazzo Orlandi in which Verdi and Strepponi lived. Giuseppina Strepponi (below) always tried to calm the diatribes that arose between the maestro and the people of Busseto.

Opposite left: the frontispiece of the original score of Rigoletto, picturing the famous quartet in the last act. The main singers at the premiere at La Fenice in 1851 were the baritone Felice Varesi, the tenor Raffaele Mirate, the soprano Teresina Brambilla, the basso Feliciano Ponz, and the contralto Annetta Casaloni.
Here alongside: Piazza San Marco in Venice in a painting by E. Budin, kept in the Le Havre Museum. After the Rigoletto premiere, the gondoliers, that same night, were already singing the famous cabaletta "La donna è mobile", which they picked up immediately.

Here below: the cover of the libretto and some costumes from Luisa Miller, staged at the San Carlo Theater in 1849 (etchings at the foot of the page). In Naples Giuseppe Verdi often found reasons to be angry, but then he would be quite glad to go back there. The maestro had dear Neapolitan friends, who for years sent him at Sant'Agata certain special cases of spaghetti. Built in 1737 at the request of Charles III of the Bourbons, in 1816 the San Carlo was destroyed by a great fire. In the 19th century its fortunes were tied to the impresario Barbaja, who brought to Naples the operas of Rossini, Bellini and Donizetti, together with such first-rate singers as Malibran, Colbran, and Lablache.

THE CENSORSHIP PERSECUTES RIGOLETTO

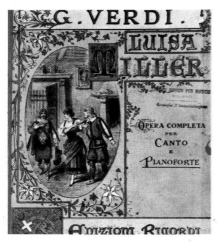

In October, 1849, Verdi had finished his new opera for the San Carlo, *Luisa Miller*, based on Schiller's tragedy. But in order to go to Naples he had to submit to the quarantine, imposed on all those who came from abroad. Therefore, the premiere was postponed until December 8, 1849. *Luisa Miller's* delicate music was received rather coldly. It was a modern opera, with realistic characters. Verdi is a musician who forges ahead and does not remain anchored to the old formulas: he needs an audience that follows him, understands him. Only the opera's repeat performances find a more attentive audience. The years of creative splendor are about to start. In the beginning of 1851, Verdi informed the management of La Fenice that the new opera, *La maledizione*, was finished. He had written it at Sant'Agata, in a mood of great exaltation. To the few people who met him, the maestro appeared unrecognizable, nervous: he walked up and down in the garden gesticulating, humming, declaiming. His genius was about to give the world one of its most powerful and enthralling operas. But before the performance there arose, once again, a serious difference with the Hapsburg censorship. The police continued to regard Verdi as an agitator, a musical rabble rouser who contributed to the anti-Austrian atmosphere. If in the past, for *I Lombardi* and *Ernani*, obstacles had been surmounted rather easily, with the passing of years an ever greater severity provoked new turns of the screw. Above all, the appearance on stage of plots against crowned heads was considered intolerable. Thus, the subject of *La Maledizione* based on Victor Hugo's *Le roi s'amuse* seemed downright scandalous to the censors, and the Royal Imperial Central Office for Public Order absolutely forbade the performance. The librettist Piave then had to change the most controversial passages, moving the action from France to Italy, and making Francis I into a libertine Duke of Mantua who troubled no one. Also the title became less grim, *Rigoletto*, and the opera was at last presented on March 11, 1851, at La Fenice, to an enthusiastic audience. But when it was performed in Rome, the censorship made so many changes that the story became almost incomprehensible. Later on, with *Un ballo in maschera*, Verdi ran into serious trouble with the police.

After twenty-one repeat performances at La Fenice, Rigoletto *was shown all over the world, except in Paris, because of the opposition of Victor Hugo who believed in his play but not in Giuseppe Verdi's music. Six years later, Hugo was persuaded to listen to* Rigoletto *and became enthusiastic about it, so much so that he declared: "I wish I too could get four characters to speak at the same time in such a way that the audience could understand their emotions!" Here, on the left, a stage set for* Rigoletto*; below: the opera's first act staged in recent years at La Scala under the direction of Margherita Wallmann, sets by Nicola Benois. Below: costumes from* Rigoletto.

Below: the entrance to the Villa at Sant'Agata in Busseto; and the garden as seen by the painter d'Avendano. The villa is still well kept and looked after even today and is open to visitors. On the walls, besides family portraits, there are pictures of Verdi's dearly beloved: Dante, Shakespeare, Manzoni, and Vittorio Emanuele II.

A GOOD PEASANT HE BELIEVED IN THE SOIL OF HIS EMILIA

In 1844, after the triumph of *Ernani*, Verdi bought a small piece of property in Le Roncole, with the not very aristocratic name of "Plugar" which in dialect means "flea nest". And immediately afterwards, in 1845, he made an even more important purchase: Palazzo Orlandi in Busseto, on the main thoroughfare. But during his Parisian stay, Verdi, serene and free, advised by Giuseppina Strepponi, a sensible woman with very good taste, the lover of nature and anxious to have a house all their own, began to think of a larger property, indeed an estate. The rental of the villa in Passy only fuelled his desire. Like a good Emilian peasant, with his first earnings Verdi did not go in for financial adventures, investing his money in stocks or speculations. He believed in a secure income from the land, his land, the land near Busseto, because he meant to breathe the air and mist of his town and hear the dialect of his people. At Villanova d'Arda, near Busseto, the property of Sant'Agata was put up for sale. It was a vast property sloping down to the Po River, rich in woods, vineyards, and water. The maestro's interest was attracted by it. The deal was handled by his father-in-law Barezzi, a passionate music-lover but a businessman first. To discuss the various possibilities, Barezzi travelled to Paris, put up by his son-in-law at an inn not far from the apartment in which Strepponi lived. Barezzi had already met her in Florence some years before, and he was glad to meet her again; when he returned to Busseto, he thanked her and sent his good wishes. In Paris Verdi and Barezzi talked and discussed for several days, eviscerating every aspect of the purchase at Sant'Agata, its utility, its virtues and defects, because when it came to business deals, accounts, Verdi was very precise and went into every detail. And so when he returned to Busseto the maestro settled the matter: on May 25, 1848, with the deed drawn up by Notary Balestra – "the exchange of the Sant'Agata property for the Pulgaro farm takes place between Maestro Verdi and the Brothers Merli" – the deal was closed.

Here alongside: a picturesque
corner of the garden at Sant'Agata
where Verdi strolled in search of
inspiration and silence. Giuseppina
grew early vegetables in the garden
and became quite adept at raising
nightingales. The maestro, to pass
the time, had bought a billiard
table for 600 lire. Below: a portrait
of Verdi during those years.

HE IS AMUSED BY THE PARODIES OF IL TROVATORE

At the premiere of Il Trovatore *in Rome, the singers were Penco, Goggi, Baucarde, Guicciardini, and Baldesi. However, to avoid the usual gossip, Verdi did not bring along Giuseppina. Facing page, top:* Il Trovatore *at La Scala, sets by Pizzi, under the direction of Giorgio De Lullo. Despite certain rather unclear passages in the libretto, Il*

Trovatore is, among Verdi's operas, the one that most fascinates today's politically committed culture. Also the young, in recent years, have returned to Verdi. Below: two sets for Il Trovatore, *the one on the right is by N. Benois, the one on the left is from Verdi's times. Right below, the libretto's cover.*

When *Il Trovatore*'s libretto was almost finished, its author, Salvatore Camarano, died. The descendant of a family of Neapolitan artists, Cammarano, at first a playwright, later devoted himself almost entirely to writing opera librettos – for Donizetti (*Lucia di Lammermoor*), Verdi (*La battaglia di Legnano*, *Alzira*, *Luisa Miller* and *Il Trovatore*), Pacini and Mercadante. He was a librettist expert at describing historical settings, conscientious and attentive to the composer's wishes. And then he died leaving *Il Trovatore* incomplete. Verdi read the news in a paper and was much shaken by it. He sent the widow one hundred ducats in addition to what had been stipulated for the writing of the libretto, then he made an agreement with the Neapolitan poet Leone Emanuele Bardare for the missing verses.

Verdi set about composing the music in April 1851 and the opera was finished in less than a year and a half. His mother, to whom he was immensely attached, died during this period. Before getting married to Carlo Verdi she had worked as a spinner. She was a good mother, modest and intimidated by the success of her son who in fact had inherited her proud spirit and indomitable will. While creating *Il Trovatore*, Verdi transferred his sorrow to the powerful character of Azucena, the gypsy so filled with primitive maternal love.

The opera was staged at the Apollo in Rome on January 19, 1853. The audience was overwhelmed, but this time the critics were harsh: "'bel canto' has been ruined", one of them wrote, "to be replaced by sobs and shouts of rage". Instead, heroic singing was born, a new thrill, a turning away from the 19th century toward more modern vocal conquests.

Il Trovatore was also a target for satire: the Neapolitan company of the famous Pulchinello Antonio Petito had fun parodying it; and in his exhilarating *Maester Pastizza*, Ferravilla introduced humorous jabs at the new opera. One evening, in Milan, Verdi himself went to the theater, happily laughed at Ferravilla's jokes and sent him a photograph with an almost Ferravillian dedication: "Your Pepin, also known as Giuseppe Verdi". While they amused Verdi, the parodies of *Il Trovatore* irritated his publisher Ricordi.

ANTONIO VASSELLI
L'EDITORE
TITO DI GIO. RICORDI

IL TROVATORE
Dramma in quattro parti di Salvadore Cammarano
POSTO IN MUSICA DAL MAESTRO
GIUSEPPE VERDI
Cavaliere della Legion d'Onore

THE HOT YEARS OF ITALIAN NATIONAL HISTORY

After the 1848-49 period of the Risorgimento, there began in 1855 the "hot years" of Italian national history. An Italian expeditionary force went to the Crimea to help the Allies who had been at war for two years. The conflict had begun in 1852 between Russia and Turkey, due to a violent dispute over the "Eastern question"; but at the same time, a harsh struggle for European supremacy was taking place amoung the great powers. So England and France had lined up against Russia on the side of Turkey. Now the Kingdom of Sardinia brought its military and political power to Crimea, hoping also in this way to redeeem the failures at Custoza and Novara. The war ended November 1, 1855, and a few months later, while the peace treaty in Paris was being signed, Cavour skillfully grafted the Italian problem on the general one of European peace. So he demonstrated that Piedmont would be in a position to handle with authority the right of independence from Austria. Italian patriotism was thus closing its ranks around the banner of Vittorio Emanuele II: Piedmont began to welcome and protect patriots; Napoleon II no longer hid his sympathy for the Italian problem; in 1857 Carlo Pisacane landed at Sapri and was immediately killed; in January 1859 the alliance between France and Piedmont was reinforced by the political marriage of Princess Clotilde, Vittorio Emanuele's daughter, to Jerome Bonaparte. Giuseppe Verdi, as was his habit, followed all these political events with tense excitement. These were his years of work, of journeys and polemics, during which his friend Emanuele Muzio kept him constantly informed on what was happening in Europe: the trial against the martyrs of Belfiore, the serious sentences against the Mazzinians in Milan, and the police measures against citizens. Muzio wrote: "The gates of Milan are still closed and nobody can go out or come in except for travelers and those who are bringing provisions to the city". In 1854 Verdi was in Paris and, although he wasn't in good health, he finished *I Vespri Siciliani*. It was presented at the Paris Opera on June 13, 1855, indeed in the climate of the Crimean War. Vittorio Emanuele's troops were fighting at the side of the French and in Paris there were protests because *I Vespri's* story actually dealt with a revolt that took place against France. At the Paris Opera there were many Italians, who had come to bestow a new triumph on Verdi's opera. So there arose again the old and unjust accusation of a political success.

Pictured on these pages are the episodes and events which disturbed and enthused Verdi's Italian heart. Opposite page: the allied commanders of the Crimean war: Alfonso Lamarmora, commander of the Italian Expedition; the Englishman, Raglan, the Frenchman Pélissier and the Turkish General Omar Pashá. Above: the battle of San Martino in 1859 in which Piedmontese soldiers, after repeated attacks, defeated the Austrians. Here at left: a portrait of General Lamarmora and a depiction of the death at Sapri of the Neapolitan patriot Carlo Pisacane.

PARIS INSPIRES THE IMMORTAL NOTES OF LA TRAVIATA

In February 1852 Verdi had attended in Paris a performance of a play in five acts which Alexander Dumas *fils* had based on his already famous novel *La dame aux camelias*. Conquered by the story, which reproduced the "dolce vita" of those days in contrast to the strict principles of bourgeois society, Verdi asked the author for a copy of the play (he received it eight months later), absorbed it, and gave it to his librettist Piave with just one recommendation: trim down the last act, too prolix. Gradually as Piave handed in the verses, Verdi set them to music. The story of Violetta was already fermenting in his heart and without hesitation the opera was written down in one creative outburst and was ready in a few months. But the audience at La Fenice on March 6, 1853 did not like *La Traviata's* "too risqué" situation, that is, did not tolerate on the moral plane seeing on stage a woman of the world, while, from the theatrical angle, it did not accept a soprano who was big and fat yet was supposed to portray a woman consumed by tuberculosis. The tenor and baritone also were not up to their parts. So the audience decreed a clear, decisive failure for Verdi's most precious and romantic opera. There had already been failures with *Un giorno di regno* in Milan and *Il Corsaro* in Trieste, but with this difference: *La Traviata* was an authentic masterpiece. The same opera with slight modifications and better singers a year later received its just recognition, still in Venice, no longer at La Fenice but at the San Benedetto theater, and quite soon began triumphing in America.

After Violetta Valéry's sad story, Verdi became excited-as we said-over the subject of *I Vespri Siciliani*. The rehearsals of the opera were disrupted by the flight of the soprano Cruvelli with her lover Baron Vigier. All of Paris laughed over this, while that farce not only angered Verdi but also Napoleon III, the person who paid the bills for the Opera Theater. *I Vespri* came to Italy at La Scala in 1856 with the title *Giovanna di Guzman*, because the censorship considered the original title controversial. The mood of the spectators was as emotionally tense as in the agitated years of *Nabucco* and *I Lombardi* before 1848, and the success was great in Milan, Turin, and Parma. In 1861, Italian unity having been achieved, the opera could be entitled *I Vespri Siciliani* in Italy too.

Above: four 17th century costumes for La Traviata: *after its initial failure, the dramatic action of the new edition was moved back two centuries.*
Below: the poster for the premiere at La Fenice. Together with La Traviata *was given the ballet* La lucerna meravigliosa *by the choreographer A. Monticini. Immediately after* La Traviata's *fiasco, the unenthusiastic baritone Varesi dared to say to Verdi as a* joke: "Condolences", and Verdi answered sharply: "Present them to yourself and your fellow singers!" Actually, the singers had contributed to the failure, since they perhaps did not really understand the characters they portrayed. At any rate, the audience also did not understand the subtle play of emotions out of which the plot was woven in this exquisite opera.

*Above: the interior of La Fenice.
The theater, inaugurated in 1792,
was rebuilt in 1836 after a fire and
restored in 1854. From 1844 to
1857 La Fenice presented the
world premieres of five of Verdi's
operas:* Ernani, Attila, Rigoletto,
La Traviata, *and* Simon
Boccanegra.
Below: La Traviata *at La Scala in
1964 with Zeffirelli's direction.*

1859, a year of victories and disappointments for the Italians. Here below: Napoleon III, French Emperor, shown at Magenta after the victory over the Austrians. Further down: Napoleon III in two satirical prints after the painful armistice of Villafranca. At foot of page: the French-Piedmontese troops,

having conquered Magenta in Lombardy in June 4, 1859, continued toward the Veneto Region where on June 24 they were victorious at the famous battles of San Martino and Solferino. Page on right: 1859 calendar depicting the traditional New Year's ball which was held at La Scala.

VILLAFRANCA COOLS ENTHUSIASM FOR NAPOLEON III

LIQUORE MONTEBELLO

BALSAMO DI MAGENTA

After the pact of alliance between France and Piedmont, the skillful Cavour set about preparing the war which would bring national unity to Italy. He began to provoke Austria, inviting Garibaldi to organize volunteers and he himself calling up troops. Until, on April 23, 1859, there arrived, as expected, Austria's ultimatum to Piedmont for general disarmament. With this threat, Austria became the aggressor state. On April 26, at Turin, the ultimatum was rejected and parliament gave the king full powers: it was war. On June 4, at Magenta there was a great battle between the French and Austrians; on the 8th of the same month Napoleon III and Vittorio Emanuele II entered Milan together, while Garibaldi's troops occupied Varese, Como, Bergamo, and Brescia.

The Austrians had retreated across the Mincio and the great army commanded by Franz Joseph was decisively beaten at San Martino and Solferino. While all Italians were thinking by now of the liberation of Venice, there came, like a lightning bolt in a clear sky, the armistice at Villafranca. Napoleon III, perturbed by the terrible spectacle of the bloody battlefields, had no intention of continuing the war. The Italians were dismayed and disappointed. In some shops, as a grave protest, appeared the portrait of Orsini, the anarchist who in January 1858 had tried to assassinate Napoleon. The annexation by Italy of the liberated regions came on the basis of a vote. On March 11 and 12, 1860, plebiscites were held in Tuscany, Parma, and Emilia-Romagna.

During those days of enthusiasm in 1859, the excitement also in Busseto and in Giuseppe Verdi's heart had been great. Back from Rome after the premiere of *Un ballo in maschera*, the maestro had been warned of a possible search at Sant'Agata. Together with Giuseppina he spent a whole night burning compromising papers, but on June 8th the Piedmontese forces chased the Austrians out of the Duchy of Parma and Verdi, at the height of enthusiasm, opened a subscription for the wounded and the orphans of the fallen, with his personal contribution of six hundred lire. Exalted by the victories of Solferino and San Martino he planned to compose a cantata in honor of Napoleon III but the unhappy pact at Villafranca cooled off the fires of his inspiration.

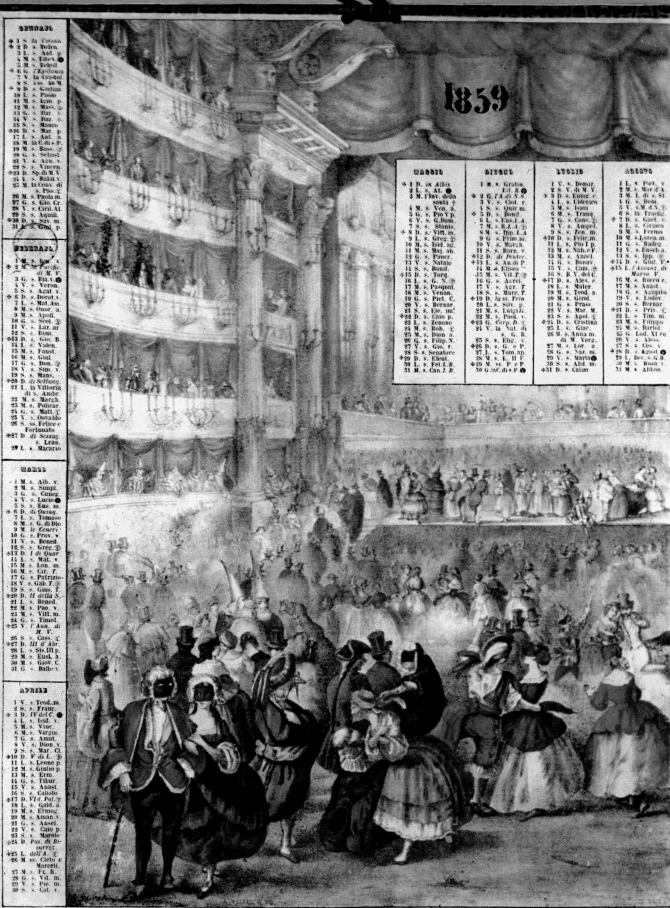

1859

Editore A. MORUZZI, Milano.   IL VEGLIONE DEL TEATRO ALLA SCALA

VERDI WOULD HAVE LIKED TO FIGHT WITH ARMS TOO

On right: Vittorio Emanuele II, in a painting preserved at the Museum of the Risorgimento in Milan. Below: on Italy's walls the slogan "Viva Verdi" and a French encampment on the bastions of Porta Vittoria in Milan (Civic Collection Bertarelli). On facing page: Napoleon III and Vittorio Emanuele II enter Milan.

In 1859 theater audiences were electrified by the turn of events. Already in January at La Scala, the spectators had jumped to their feet at the chorus of "Guerra, guerra!" in Bellini's *Norma*, to which the Austrian officers in their white tunics replied, shouting: "You shall have it, dogs!" And in February 1859 at Naples Verdi had become the symbol of the Italian spirit also on walls and posters, because "Viva Verdi" (Long live Verdi), from the letters of the name, was understood by all to mean "Viva Vittorio Emanuele Re d'Italia" (Long live Vittorio Emanuele King of Italy).

After Vittorio Emanuele II and Napoleone III entered Milan to a triumphant welcome, La Scala, which had been closed for some months, was reopened, and before an enthusiastic audience the two sovereigns attended a vocal and instrumental concert in their honor. During those days Verdi from Sant'Agata sent a significant letter to his friend Countess Maffei: "I can hardly believe it. Who would have thought of so much generosity on the part of our allies! As for myself I confess and declare my very great *mea culpa* because I did not believe the French would come to Italy and certainly not that they would shed their blood for us without some idea of conquest. On the first point I was mistaken; I hope and pray to be mistaken on the second, that Napoleon will not repudiate the proclamation of Milan. Then I will worship him as I worship Washington and even more, and blessing the great nation I will gladly tolerate all their *blague*, their insolent *politesse*, and the scorn they have for everything that is not French".

Several times Verdi would have liked to join the combatants, offering a physical contribution besides his spiritual one to the cause of freedom, but from forty to fifty he did not enjoy good health, chiefly because of certain stomach ailments. "What could I do", he said pessimistically, "when I'm not capable of sustaining a three mile march, my head can't bear five minutes of sun, and a little wind and humidity give me a sore throat and send me to bed sometimes for weeks. My miserable make-up! Good for nothing!" This time too he had to be satisfied with following his country's great events from a distance; but his friends, and among them Maestro Mariani, continued to keep him informed about political and military matters, sending him letters which were sometimes ten pages long, with copies of entire official bulletins and the newspapers' comments.

About his own political ideas Verdi declared: "Colors don't frighten me, but I fear intolerance and violence. What's more, I have believed and will always believe that changes in the world have been brought about by men of genius. I expect that those in charge of public affairs will be citizens of great commitment and impeccable honesty".
In 1860 Cavour favored Verdi's election as a deputy. In parliament the maestro sat next to Quintino Sella. In 1875 Verdi was nominated senator for life. Here at left: Piazza del Duomo illuminated for the king's arrival in 1859.

Below: Costumes for Simon Boccanegra. *For this opera too Verdi composed innovative music, but the verdict of the audience at La Fenice was negative. On right: Simon Boccanegra's libretto and the poster for* Un ballo in maschera *at the Manzoni Theater in Milan.*

DELIRIUM IN ROME FOR UN BALLO IN MASCHERA

Opposite page, top: scene from Simon Boccanegra *in a drawing that appeared in "Illustrazione Italiana" in February, 1881. Verdi wrote to Maffei that the opera had been "a fiasco almost as great as that of* La Traviata. *I thought that I had done something acceptable, but now it appears that I was under a misapprehension".*

In the years around the second War of Independence, Verdi composed two important operas: *Simon Boccanegra*, performed at La Fenice on January 12, 1857, with results that can only be called mediocre (twenty-four years had to pass before the opera was revised, and it is the new edition that is still performed today) and *Un ballo in maschera* which on the contrary had, and rightly, a delirious success in Rome, because of its enthralling musical quality (a kind of "condensed version" of the now famous trilogy *Rigoletto*, *La Traviata*, and *Il Trovatore*), and – this time too – because of the political obstacles that the opera's story had to overcome. Adapter more than author of the libretto of *Un ballo in maschera* was the Friulian lawyer and poet Antonio Somma, former superintendent of the Comunale Theater in Triest, author of plays in which Gustavo Modena and Adelaide Ristori performed, and finally fervent patriot. It seems strange that this poet, criticized and even derided for such verses as "Sento l'orma dei passi spietati" (I hear the tracks of the merciless footsteps) or "Raggiante di pallor" (In her radiant pallor – not quite as bad as is generally said) was so esteemed by Verdi that the maestro in 1853 wrote to him: "Nothing for me better, nothing dearer, than to join my name to your great one".

With the story of *Un ballo in maschera*, based on Scribe, Verdi again ran into difficulties with the censorship, this time Bourbon, because the opera was to be performed in Naples. First the title, *Una vendetta in domino* had to be changed (the police did not care for vendettas or curses), and subsequently drastic changes in setting and characters were imposed. In fact among them was Gustave II of Sweden assassinated on stage in the opera for personal reasons. Gustave of Sweden was the cousin of Francis I: hence the plot against the king's life seemed to the censors even more objectionable. But Verdi, inflexible as ever, did not accept the mutilations, and rejected the audience granted him at Naples by King Ferdinando. Thanks to diplomatic maneuvers by impresario Jacovacci, who could boast of authoritative friends in Vatican circles, *Un ballo in maschera* was staged with few changes on February 17, 1859, not in Naples but at the Apollo Theater in Rome.

Below: Stage settings by Ferrario for Simon Boccanegra and Un ballo in maschera. *The latter had already been set to music by Auber and Mercadante, but this did not discourage Verdi who saw in Eugene Scribe's play powerful, sure-fire theatrical material. The love duet in the second act was to be one of Verdi's most fascinating* pages. *Gabriele D'Annunzio will consider this opera: "The most dramatic of dramatic operas". The premiere of* Un ballo in maschera, *despite the bad singers, had great success: during the repeat performances people paid fabulous prices for the boxes and admissions were seven times the regular price.*

1859 IS ALSO THE YEAR OF HIS MARRIAGE TO STREPPONI

A clause in the preliminary talks at Villafranca established that various regions in Italy, among them the Duchy of Parma, must decide with a free plebiscite whether or not to unite with Piedmont. At Parma too the outcome of the vote was for unity and Giuseppe Verdi, together with another four citizens, was chosen to bring the news to the king. Verdi was a republican, but he liked Vittorio Emanuele II because he had always kept his word and at that moment was the right man to unify Italy. So Verdi reached Turin with the delegates on September 15, 1859, and the audience with the king was cordial, almost informal. Cavour too, who had resigned in protest over Villafranca, was very happy to meet Verdi at Leri, where he had retired. When rumors spread in Parma about a possible return of the Austrian Archduchess Maria Luisa, a territorial militia was hastily set up at Busseto and Verdi ordered from Genoa 170 rifles of English manufacture, paying for them out of his own

pocket. But the decisive results of a second plebiscite in March 1869 rendered these measures unnecessary. When calm returned, the king visited Parma. The people of Busseto gave him the gift of a new cannon and Verdi declared himself happy †that the money had not been wasted.

But 1859 was not only that of the Second War of Independence and *Un ballo in maschera*, it was also the year of Verdi's marriage to Giuseppina Strepponi. After a long period of living together happily, the hasty marriage was celebrated in of Our Lady of Geneva at Collanges-sous-Salère (in Savoy, still part of Piedmont) on April 29, 1859, by his friend and rector of the church, Abbot Mermillod. On that same day the Austrians crossed the Ticino, starting a war. When her short, intense career as a singer ended, Giuseppina Strepponi began the career of companion, secretary and faithful adviser. It was she who had always wanted to put off the marriage with Verdi, not feeling worthy of him, as she said. Her private life, before falling in love with the maestro and living with him, had been quite free and adventurous. She did not have any children with Verdi, and so one day she will write to her Giuseppe: "… we shall not have them perhaps because the Lord is punishing me for my sins: not having children with me, do not give me the sorrow of having them with some other woman".

40

Above, left: the people of Milan were disappointed by the news of the armistice of Villafranca (painting by Jerome Induno at Milan's Museum of the Risorgimento). Here at left: Verdi's and Strepponi's license for the marriage which took place that year. Above: Verdi brings the king the news that the Duchy of Parma has united with Italy (drawing by Edoardo Matania). In print alongside: Camillo Benso di Cavour on his farm at Leri (near Trino, in the Vercelli area) to which he retired after the peace of Villafranca. Verdi, when he became a deputy, always devotedly followed the liberal policy of Cavour, one of the eminent men for whom he had great esteem.

HE SWUNG FROM BRUSQUE MANNERS TO MOMENTS OF GREAT GRACIOUSNESS

Verdi had a timid and taciturn character, when young his manners were downright boorish. But when he moved to Milan and experienced his initial fame he entered salons without any shyness and had polite and even gracious manners. His demeanor was serious, imperious, demanding respect; his way of joking with friends was a trifle heavy-handed, and with the ladies he alternated brusque manners with moments of graciousness and gaiety which fascinated them. Many of the prima donnas who sang in his operas were rumored to be his mistresses, but nobody would have dared to speak of it in his presence, despite the fact that a relationship with Countess Gina della Somiglia and another with Appiani were matters of common gossip.

The thought of God was rooted in Verdi's mind and conscience, but his religion was not that of the Church. Also politically he was against the Church and feared its temporal domination. He was a free thinker. But he was a fervent reader of the Bible, which he admired. After it in the list of favorite books came Shakespeare's dramas and the poems of Ariosto.

In matters of work he was intransigent, hard, obstinate. The librettists always had to give in to him, he was adamant also with his publisher Ricordi, and inflexible with the singers.

He was touchy, sensitive. When he was named Commander of the Crown, having heard that the Minister of Education Emilio Broglio had remarked that there were no composers after Rossini and Meyerbeer, he disdainfully returned the decoration. But, in truth, he did not care for that sort of recognition. When a newspaper reported that the government intended to confer on him the title of Marquis of Busseto he telegraphed Minister Martini: "Asking you to do your best to prevent. My gratitude much greater if no title is given". When in his later years he went to luxurious hotels and grand mansions, Verdi no longer was the peasant from Le Roncole, he had distinguished manners, dressed well, wore fine linen, enjoyed a refined cuisine and had many servants. Making fun of him, Giuseppina used to say: "You a peasant were born a prince. Your mother must have cheated on your father when those Russian troops passed through Le Roncole".

Per la scala del balcone
Presto andate via di quà

ALWAYS SEVERE WITH THE INTERPRETERS OF HIS OPERAS

M. Barbieri-Nini

Maria Waldmann

Carolina Barbot

Felice Varesi

Giorgio Ronconi

Gaetano Fraschini

Luigi Lablache

Teresina Stolz

Verdi was always severe with the singers who played in his operas, whether they be called Giorgio Ronconi, Johanna Sophie Loewe, Erminia Frezzolini, Maria Waldmann, Eugenia Tadolini, Victor Maurel or Francesco Tamagno, all prestigious names considered to this day exemplary figures in the history of European *bel canto*. The only testimony that has come down to us from those days are a few records cut in the very early years of the 20th century by the baritone Maurel and the tenors Tamagno and Garbin, technically too defective for us to make a comparison with the voices of the modern period. But from the interpretation of some parts of *Otello* which Tamagno has left

on a record, one can well understand why Verdi was so satisfied by the excellent vocal qualities of the legendary tenor, but not with the superficiality with which he interpreted the characters. Verdi insisted that every singer sing and act in complete humility, without playing the great star, fully at the service of the music and the character, coming as close as possible to perfection. During a rehearsal of *Macbeth* he insisted, for example, that the baritone Varesi and the soprano Barbieri-Nini repeat their duet for the nth time. The baritone lost his patience and snapped: "But we already rehearsed it one hundred and fifty times, by God!" "You won't say that in a half hour", the maes-

E. Frezzolini-Poggi

Eugenia Tadolini

Jenny Lind

Teresa Brambilla

Adelina Patti

Marietta Brambilla

A. Borghi-Mamo

Sophie Loewe

Maria Piccolomini

Victor Maurel

Sofia Cruvelli

Rosina Penco

Luigia Boccabadati

Maria Sass

Prospero Derivis

tro answered sharply, "because by then it will be one hundred and fifty-one!"

The interpreter *par excellence* of Verdi's operas was the very beautiful Teresa Stolz, a Czech soprano. Before her, her twin sisters Fanny and Lidia had become famous, connected both in art and in their emotional lives with the Italian maestro Luigi Ricci (co-author of the opera *Crispino e la comare*). Ricci then married Lidia, but with Fanny he had a child who was named Luigi Ricci-Stolz and became Teresa's heir. Stolz, who settled in Italy, making her debut at La Scala in 1865 with great success in Verdi's *Giovanna d'Arco*, had a powerful voice with a wide range (even if a trifle uneven), together with style, technique, and an unparalleled artistic temperament. At the end of her career she opened in Milan a famous salon frequented by every artist in Europe. Verdi was also strict with the orchestra. When at La Scala a contrabass player stated that it was impossible to execute a certain passage, the maestro sent a telegram to Parma and called to Milan a certain Pinetti, also born at Le Roncole. When they saw that peasant type the cultivated musicians in the orchestra laughed, but Pinetti performed the protested passage without difficulty. Verdi simply said: "Gentlemen, that's how we play in Parma".

HE BECAME A CLOSE FRIEND OF THE AUTHORS OF HIS LIBRETTOS

A most trusted and lifelong friend, unconditionally at Verdi's side, was Maestro Emanuele Muzio. He too had been helped with his studies by Barezzi and the Monte di Pietà in Busseto, and besides being Verdi's only pupil he was his secretary, his confidant, messenger, and even nurse. He helped him copy scores, take care of the correspondence, and proved most useful by listening to the music of other composers about which he reported in the most accurate technical terms. Muzio was also active as orchestra conductor in Europe and America and had, among his voice pupils, Adelina Patti. He died in Paris, in 1890. Verdi also offered his esteem and friendship to the journalist Opprandino Arrivabene, attracted by his modesty and his disinterested love for his country and the arts.

The bond between Verdi and Francesco Maria Piave rested not only on their work but also on true affection. Gifted with theatrical instinct and dramatic power, Piave wrote about sixty librettos and, among these, he prepared for Verdi: *Ernani, I due Foscari, Macbeth, Il Corsaro, Stifellio, Rigoletto, La Traviata, Aroldo* (a remake of *Stiffelio*), *Simon Boccanegra, La Forza del Destino*. When Piave was stricken by paralysis, Verdi helped his family and had him removed from the public ward to a room for paying patients. A unique personage among Verdi's librettists was Temistocle Solera, the author of *Oberto* who, in his clashes with the maestro was always forced to give in despite his very strong personality. Solera, in 1850, abandoned literature for a life of adventure: first he entered the secret service of Napoleon III, and then he was in charge of the repression of brigandry in Calabira, after that he became the chief of police in Florence, Palermo, Bologna, and Venice, until he was summoned to Egypt to organize the secret service in that country. Lastly, he had several love affairs at the court of Isabella in Spain, and poor returned to Milan thanks only to a collection made by Countess Maffei. Antonio Ghislanzoni, the librettist of *Aida*, was a prolific poet. First a baritone, journalist, poet of the "scapigliatura Lombarda", he later wrote eighty-five librettos for the greatest musicians of his time, from Verdi to Ponchielli, Catalani to Gomes. The verses of Ghislanzoni, Somma, and Piave are often considered inferior. Only in his old age did Verdi have the support of a truly modern poet, Arrigo Boito.

Opposite page: Fuori Porta Orientale, *in Milan (by A. Fermini). Below: Piave, Muzio, Ghislanzoni, and Somma. This page, above: piazza of the Duomo in 1862 (Milan Museum). On the left: square of La Scala and the Casino dei Nobili (Society Club); Andrea Maffei and his wife Countess Clara. Clara Maffei's celebrated salon was attended by Verdi, Donizetti, Balzac, Liszt, and Massimo d'Azeglio. In Verdi's letters the name of Chiarina or Clara Maffei is often mentioned: from these letters it is possible to reconstruct episodes of the maestro's life which otherwise would have been lost. On the advice of Verdi and Manzoni, Clara Maffei had separated from her husband Andrea, a poet from Trento, handsome and elegant but too devoted to women and gambling. When, in 1886, Clara Maffei was struck by meningitis, Verdi rushed from Montecatini to her bedside just in time to see her die on July 13, 1886.*

HE WROTE LETTERS TO HIS FRIENDS AND SIGNED THEM WITH THE NAME OF ONE OF HIS DOGS

Often as many as four or five years in Verdi's life passed between the writing of one opera and the next and in these lapses of time Verdi was again the average man, looking after his estates, travelling, reading and hunting. Animals played an important part in his emotions and his leisure. He loved horses, birds and above all dogs. On walks through the fields it was easy to meet him with his Great Danes while a parrot whom Strepponi had taught to sing "La donna è mobile" even enjoyed the privilege of going on carriage rides with his masters. But Verdi's and Strepponi's true love was a small Maltese dog, named Lulu, who was part of the family like a person and often went with them on their travels through Italy and abroad. He was even taken to St. Petersburg for the premiere of *La Forza del Destino*. The famous orchestra conductor Mariani personally intervened to obtain a passport for Lulu. When Lulu died, Verdi wrote to Mariani this sad and heartfelt letter: "A serious misfortune has befallen us and grieves us dreadfully, Lulu, our poor Lulu has died! Poor little beast! The true friend, the faithful, inseparable companion of almost six years

of our life! So affectionate! So beautiful!". Lulu was later replaced by another dog, Black, who also became Verdi's inseparable companion when he worked composing. While Verdi sat at the piano, Black curled up beside him and watched him for hours, as if to assist him. Interesting are the letters that Verdi wrote to his friend Arrivabene pretending they were written by Black to keep him informed about the new operas the maestro was composing, he being the lucky witness.

It is know that all his life Verdi thought of setting to music Shakespeare's *King Lear*: Somma had written at least two acts for him and the music was sketched out at Sant'Agata so that in 1856 discussions began with the San Carlo in Naples for its performance. The musical sketches for *Re Lear* eventually ended up in the fire together with other unfinished music, as Verdi had instructed in his will. One can therefore say that his dogs, Lulu and Black, were the only ones to hear the notes created by their master for Shakespeare's drama.

It is, nevertheless, claimed that a few pages written for *Re Lear* were later incorporated by Verdi into *La Forza del Destino*.

Opposite page: Verdi plays with his Great Danes in the garden at Sant'Agata (watercolor in the Ricordi collection). Left: a corner of the garden with varied and rare plants, the same as it was in Verdi's time. On his estate, the maestro had also built a small lake on which he sometimes went rowing.

On the left: Giuseppina Strepponi's bedroom. The oval on the wall to the right contains a portrait Palizzi painted of the parrot that so amused the Verdi couple during their leisure hours at Sant'Agata. Here above: the lively image of Lulu (painting by Palizzi), Verdi's favorite dog. Lulu was buried among the bushes under the maestro's and Giuseppina's rooms, so that every morning, when they opened the shutters, they would remember him. On the stone was carved: "To one of my most trusted friends". Wagner also loved dogs: when one of his died he wore mourning for days on end.

AT ST. PETERSBURG LA FORZA DEL DESTINO EARNED HIM 22,000 RUBLES

While looking for a story for an opera to be staged at the Imperial Theater in St. Petersburg in 1862, Verdi came upon a famous Spanish drama *Don Alvaro o la fuerza del sino* by Don Angel de Saveedra, Duke of Rivas. The author, who had been a cavalry officer and an ambassador at the court of Naples, was also a good man of letters. Verdi defined the story as "powerful, singular, vast", and set to work immediately with alacrity, fascinated above all by the vicissitudes of the unfortunate character of Alvaro. When in January 1862 *La Forza del destino* was completed, Verdi, together with Giuseppina, went to St. Petersburg to oversee the rehearsals. The performance, however, had to be postponed due to the illness of one of the singers and Verdi used the opportunity to take a trip to France and England (on that occasion his *Hymn of the Nations* was performed in London). He then spent the summer in Italy doing the orchestration for *La Forza del destino*, and this was unusual because, habitually, the maestro saw to the orchestration during rehearsals. On August 25, 1862, he left again for St. Petersburg where he arrived, with his wife, in the middle of September, after a stop in Paris. He also stayed in Moscow for four days; he visited the Kremlin and, incognito, attended a performance of *Il Trovatore*, but, recognized, he was applauded enthusiastically and called to the proscenium. All along, the "unsociable" Verdi allowed himself to be lured into society, accepted dinner invitations, went to parties, surprised by Russian friendliness, so very different from that of Paris.

At last, on November 10, 1862, *La Forza del destino* opened at the Imperial Theater of St. Petersburg. It was a great success, but not a triumph. Czar Alexander bestowed on the composer the Order of St. Stanislas, but there were also polemics because Verdi had earned 22,000 rubles while Russian composers, for the same kind of effort, received 500. On top of this, the Czar had put at Verdi's disposal the chorus members of his Guard regiments, and the management of the Imperial Theater had budgeted two hundred thousand francs, an expense that was abundantly covered by the enormous box office receipts. On the whole, *La Forza del destino* was considered too long and disjointed. It was, however, praised for the considerable improvement of Verdi's orchestration. For the La Scala performance (1869) Verdi reworked several parts of the opera, changed the fourth finale, and replaced the prelude with the famous symphony.

Far left: the score for voice and piano of La Forza del destino; *the Florentine tenor Giuseppe Fancelli in the habit of Don Alvaro; a set by N. Benois for the La Scala production of* La Forza del destino *in the 1965-66 season.*

Left: desk set given by Czar to Verdi at opera's premiere.

Above: Verdi in Russia wearing fur coat and cossack hat; below: the maestro on a troika with friends. Strepponi had made sure that their journey to Russia would have the comfort of 120 bottles of bordeaux, 20 bottles of champagne, provisions of cheese, salami, tagliatelle and a sizeable supply of rice because besides being a gourmet Verdi knew how to prepare an excellent risotto. In 1863 La Forza del destino *was triumphantly received in Spain, where the maestro granted himself a vacation and visited Madrid, Seville, Cordoba, and Granada but was disappointed by the Escorial.*

VERDI PERSONALLY MANAGED HIS FARM AND HIS ESTATES

Verdi's and Giuseppina's refuge was the villa at Sant'Agata: after their travels, after the famous premieres, and after the sojourns in Genoa, they always returned to it to rest mentally and recover physically, to draw new inspiration from it and enjoy the quiet of nature and their contact with it. Love for the countryside was deeply rooted in Giuseppe Verdi's nature. His ancestors were from Ponte Taro, a few miles from Parma; they had breathed the same air, dealing in cattle and working the soil. At the end of the 18th century Verdi's grandfather already lived in Le Roncole, with no less than seven children to support. Bach, Mozart, and Beethoven, to mention just a few, came from families of more or less celebrated musicians, they received from their forebears the gift of music, since adolescence they enjoyed in the home both studies and examples. None of this was given to Verdi at birth, he received his gifts from Providence. But his love for the soil he indeed inherited from his peasant parents and grandparents and held it most dear. He personally managed his estates – he rose at dawn, supervised all activities, kept track of the harvests, closely followed restoration work and additional building at the villa, looked after the horses and trained them. He personally directed the digging of an artesian well, and he always fought peasant ignorance by introducing technical improvements on his farm. Already in his sixties and very rich, he was seen one day in Cremona at the weekly cattle market, bargaining with the dealers. This is how the maestro described his Sant'Agata estate to Countess Maffei: "It is impossible to find a place uglier than this but on the other hand it is impossible for me to find anywhere I could live in greater freedom. Besides, this silence gives me time to think, and then never having to see a uniform of any color is certainly a good thing!" And to his friend Arrivabene: "If you tell me that *Don Carlos* is worth nothing I care not at all, but if you dispute my ability as a mason I will take it in bad part".

Especially in the winter time the hours in the villa at Sant'Agata were monotonous, muffled. The only excitement was the arrival of the afternoon mail, the only tie to the outside world. Sometimes husband and wife went for an outing on foot or by carriage, but only rarely would they be seen in Busseto.

Illustrations below: Verdi with his horses at the villa in Sant'Agata. A passionate horse-lover, in 1857 the maestro wrote to his friend, the sculptor Luccardi: "You, who are from the Friuli, live in the Friuli or close to the Friuli, tell me, then, if it would be possible to obtain two horses, of the largest breed, able to draw a carriage, able to take long journeys and, at the same time, beautiful and genuine…"
And to his friend he liked to say: "Horses are like women, they must please their owner".

FAMILY MEMENTOS PRESERVED IN THE PEACE OF SANT'AGATA

At Sant'Agata the maestro used his bedroom also as his study, where he locked himself in so as not to be disturbed by anybody. Right next to it was Giuseppina's room: to her he often turned, waking her in the middle of the night to get her immediate opinion on a phrase he had just composed. Loving and competent, Strepponi would sit by his side and, accompanied on the piano, she would sing the piece so that he could immediately judge what the effect would be on stage. For Verdi, a theatrical genius, those few hints were enough.

One of the maestro's habitual goals at Sant'Agata was the Vidalenzo cemetery, not far from the villa, where his parents were laid to rest. His father had died on January 14, 1867 when Verdi was in Paris for the rehearsals of *Don Carlos*. Overcome by his loss, he remained secluded in his hotel room for several days, unable to resume his work. At the time of his death Carlo Verdi was 82 years old. During his life he would have very much liked to manage his famous son's estates, but Giuseppe chose not to entrust him with that heavy responsibility.

That same year, on July 21, also Verdi's father-in-law and benefactor, Antonio Barezzi, passed away. The maestro and Strepponi, who spent those months in Genoa, just managed to rush to his bedside. The farewells were unimaginably pathetic. As he was dying Barezzi insisted that his Pepin play for him on the piano the melody which had always been his favorite, the chorus "Va pensiero sull'ali dorate". Verdi, weeping, did as he was asked. Then Barezzi raised his hand as if to bless the maestro and whispered: "Oh, my Verdi!... and he passed away pronouncing that modest yet perfect sentence of admiration.

Verdi, having returned for a few days to Sant'Agata for Barezzi's death, imparted the news to his friend Arrivabene with these words: "Poor signor Antonio, my second father, the man who loved me so much, is no longer. His great age does not mitigate my immense sorrow. Poor signor Antonio! If there is a second life he must see that I loved him and that I am grateful to him for all he has done for me. He died in my arms, and I have the comfort of never have done anything to grieve him".

Left: the poplar walk in the garden at Sant'Agata (watercolor in Ricordi collection). Here below: four pictures of the villa: a small sitting room with 18th century furniture, a view of the garden, Giuseppina's bedroom (near the bed, on night table, a reliquary presented by the Emperor of Austria), a corner of the formal red sitting room. In 1868, having realized that their marriage was barren, Verdi and Strepponi decided to adopt the small daughter of a cousin, Maria Verdi, and to send her away to school at the Collegio della Provvidenza in Turin. The required documentation included their marriage certificate, only on that occasion was it possible to know the exact details of their union. In time Maria was to marry the notary Carrara. She remained with the maestro all his life and became his sole heir, with the proviso that she keep up the villa and the garden at Sant'Agata and "maintain all the meadows in their present condition".

Palazzo Doria in Genoa where Verdi lived after his break with Angelo Mariani; below: bestowal of the Genoese citizenship on Verdi. In medallions, Maestro Mariani surrounded by the performers of Lohengrin *in Bologna, after the quarrel with Verdi. Opposite page: soprano Teresina Stolz in a painting preserved at the La Scala Museum.*

When in Paris, Verdi liked to spend his Saturday evenings at the house of Gioacchino Rossini (photo below). One evening Rossini decided the attraction should be a performance of the quartet from Rigoletto, *and he himself accompanied the singers at the piano. Among them were the celebrated Patti, Alboni, Gardoni, Delle Sedia. Right: the theater of the Opera. Below: introductory chords written by Rossini during a musical evening in 1863, in order to interrupt the guests' conversation and attract attention to the trio of Verdi's* Attila *which begins without introductory chords (La Scala's Theatrical Museum). Although Verdi often polemicized with Paris and the Parisians, he kept returning there for a few months every year.*

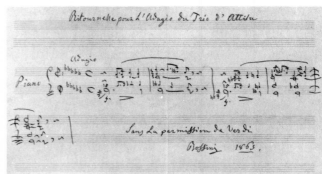

EMOTIONS AND FINANCIAL CONSIDERATIONS MINGLE IN A PAINFUL AFFAIR

Among Italian cities Verdi loved above all Genoa, which, due to the reserved character of its people, made it possible for him to live quite isolated. As a rule, he resided at the Hotel Croce di Malta, but since he and his wife found the climate agreeable, in 1866 he rented an apartment in Palazzo Sauli on the same floor as soprano Teresa Stolz and Maestro Angelo Mariani, who lived together as husband and wife. His windows looked out on the sea and all around rose dense and blossoming trees.

The two couples were very close. Verdi held Maestro Mariani in particular esteem. Only to him did he grant the freedom to interpret some of his operas in a subjective way, that is, "to add something of his own". Mariani, in fact, was a precursor of the modern conductor: he did not execute passively but re-created the composer's spirit through his own personality. Verdi appreciated Mariani, but at the same time he had also fallen in love with Teresina Stolz. And one day, suddenly, the irreparable took place. What actually occurred, the biographers have not been able to ascertain. It was said that the quarrel was provoked by Verdi's passion, but no proof of this exists. Stolz, in any case, always remained a friend of the composer and of Strepponi. The break with Mariano was given an interpretation that mixed emotions with matters of money. Stolz wanted to legalize her situation with Mariani but he refused; at that point, Stolz demanded that he return a large amount of money, forty-two thousand lire, that she had entrusted to him during their intimate relationship. Mariani did not comply and to Verdi, who intervened on Teresa's behalf, he said that he had lost the money in a financial speculation. Verdi who was endowed with the greatest sense of honor and scrupulousness in money matters, was indignant and broke with Mariani who, out of revenge, joined the ranks of the Wagnerians. During those years the Wagnerians were becoming boisterous and polemical also with the support of such intellectuals as Panzacchi, Carducci and Boito. In 1871, in fact, Maestro Angelo Mariani conducted in Bologna the Italian premiere of *Lohengrin*, achieving a great success. Verdi himself attended one of the repeat performances and was much applauded.

Mariani died in June, 1873, at the age of fifty-two. At the news, Verdi exclaimed: "What a loss for art!"

DOES THE MUSIC OF DON CARLOS BEAR WAGNER'S IMPRINT?

Verdi was not only accused of following Meyerbeer's theories, but also of Wagnerian tendencies: this harsh criticism reached him in Paris in March, 1867, at the premier of *Don Carlos*. But it was a false, gratuitous accusation, and he rightly resented it. Certainly, Verdi had listened to Wagner's operas, just as he had become acquainted with those of the composers who had preceded him and those of his contemporaries; and from all of them, including Wagner, he must have assimilated something. Verdi, furthermore, disapproved of all aesthetics entertained consciously, he was an instinctive person. Therefore, whenever he was accused of Wagnerian tendencies he always decisively denied having followed any theory whatsoever in composing *Don Carlos*. It is irrelevant, he said at the time, to know whether *Don Carlos* is part of a method, what matters is knowing whether it is good or bad music. When Richard Wagner died in 1883, this is how Verdi commented on the news: "Sad, sad, sad: Wagner has died. Reading the communication yesterday I was, I'm about to say, terrified by it. A great personality has disappeared: a name which leaves a most powerful mark on the history of art!". Wagner had not been as generous to Verdi; speaking about Italian opera he used to dispose of it with the words "Donizetti & Co."

Wagner's Italian publishers had been the Luccas, husband and wife, who, conversely, detested Verdi's music. Indissolubly tied to Verdi's name, on the other hand, are the Ricordi publishers, who towards the end of the 18th century had come from Spain and struck deep roots in Milan. Giovanni Ricordi, copyist and theatrical prompter, at the beginning of the 19th century gradually acquired ownership of scores, went to Leipzig to learn the art of publishing from Breitkopf & Härtel, and in 1808 founded Casa Ricordi. Soon Giovanni obtained the rights to operas by Rossini, Bellini, Donizetti and to Verdi's *Nabucco* and *I Lombardi*. He died a few days after the failure of *La Traviata* and the publishing house was inherited by his son Tito (1811-1888), a good musician with the mind of an industrialist. Tito, in time, acquired from Verdi the rights to *Un ballo in maschera*, *La Forza del destino*, *Don Carlos*, *Aida*, *Otello*. He was succeeded by the most accomplished of his sons, Giulio (1840-1912), a modern man with varied interests, a journalist, patriot, composer, who gave new impetus to the publishing house, always remaining faithful to Verdi and helping Giacomo Puccini during his formative years.

Opposite page: three moments in Don Carlos, *in G. Gonin's drawings.*
Above: a scene from Don Carlos *by Wakevicz at La Scala in 1963.*
Left: another scene of the opera, preserved at La Scala's Theatrical Museum. Despite the adverse reviews, Theophile Gautier, the French writer, was among the few to support Don Carlos *and to always defend all of Verdi's work. Also Rossini, reigning spirit of opera, openly declared that in his opinion Verdi was the only living composer capable of writing a "grand opera".*

Photograph below: a view of Verdi's study-bedroom at Sant'Agata. Visible on the desk, a terracotta urchin sculpted by Vincenzo Gemito. On the top shelf, three precious Sicilian figurines, also in terracotta, from the Caltagirone school.

VERDI WAS ALSO A GREAT DIRECTOR

In April, 1880, a petition by the Milanese demanded that, in the lobby of La Scala, a statue of Verdi be placed next to those of Donizetti and Rossini. The statue, sculpted by Barzaghi, was unveiled October 25, 1881 (the ceremony in the sketch at left). Verdi, however, did not attend the unveiling and deplored that so much publicity had been given to his name. Below: the flap-top desk at which the maestro stood to compose when he was tired of sitting at the piano. On it, the manuscript of Aida. Below: the piano used by Verdi from Rigoletto until his death.

In 1869 Verdi had been invited by the Khedive of Egypt to write an opera for the new Cairo Theater, on the occasion of the opening of the Suez Canal. The maestro declined at first but when, in Paris, impresario Camille du Locle, his friend and collaborator, got him to read the synopsis of a grandiose Egyptian tale of love and war, Verdi immediately perceived the possibilities the opera offered and accepted the commission. Author of the subject was the French egyptologist Auguste Edouard Mariette, but several details, including the final scene, were suggested by Verdi himself. Ghislanzoni enthusiastically agreed to write the verses of the libretto and, together with Tito Ricordi, he went to Sant'Agata to come to an agreement with Verdi. The contract was signed and even before the libretto was finished, Verdi began to compose so that words and music came into being together. Verdi had innate talents as a theatrical creator, as a director, as one would say today. And in composing the new opera, *Aida*, he also invented the trumpets that were to emphasize the triumph of Radames' Egypt over Amonasro's Ethiopians. It was his habit always to follow the staging of the premieres, down to the smallest detail, with unquestionable scrupulousness and flair. He began by making difficulties about the librettos: if the poet had not interpreted his intentions, he insisted that the verses be changed and adjusted until they fit the meaning of the music perfectly; he shifted emphases and substituted words to obtain greater intensity and ease of musical expression. Above all, theatrical genius that he was, and merciless with his own music, he eliminated cabalettas or cavatinas that seemed to interfere with the dramatic development or slow down the rhythm of the performance – all this to the great irritation of his librettists and the amazed horror of his singers. For a better rendition of the sounds, Verdi began to improve the distribution of the orchestra, complement it, add fullness to it, requesting on stage greater attention to the design of the scenery, the disposition of the lights, the general production and organization. He told the singers how to move, gave instructions for wigs and costumes, even set down the best positioning of doors, windows, and furnitures. Everything, in short, which in modern times is the work and province of the director.

Below: triumphal scene of Aida at La Scala in 1963, as directed by Zeffirelli. Aida, Verdi's most spectacular opera, is to this day, the "piece de resistance" of every opera season, particularly in the open air, where hundreds of warriors, dancing slaves, horses and elephants can be moved about on stage.

Opposite page: Verdi conducts Aida in Paris, in 1878. While the opera triumphed all over Europe, the maestro agreed to supervise its production only at Parma and Naples. Also in the case of Aida, Verdi was accused, not only of Wagnerian influences, but of having repeated Wagner's

mistakes: the originality of the opera, however, is essentially Italian. Its exotic coloration has always had great impact on audiences. Opposite page: the first libretto of Aida with many other mementos, preserved at La Scala's Theatrical Museum.

MULTICOLORED CROWDS AND ENTHUSIASM AT AIDA'S OPENING IN CAIRO

Aida was ready at the end of 1870, but the Franco-Prussian war delayed its production. The opera's scenery and costumes were in fact in Paris under siege. The French had surrendered at Sedan and the capital was held in the vise of Bismark's troops: without food, in January, 1871, it fell. It was during the days of Sedan, in 1870, that Verdi, responsive as always to military events, composed with great élan the march of *Aida* and sent the two thousand francs he had received as an advance for the opera to his friend Du Locle for the French wounded. Also in Italy the political situation was unstable: in 1870 there was the Breach of Porta Pia and the year after, the king entered Rome. Verdi followed the events with anxious interest. Finally it became possible for *Aida* to open at the khedival theater in Cairo, on December 24, 1871. Angelo Mariani had been approached to conduct on the first night, but his break with Verdi had already taken place and, after asking for an execessive fee, the conductor claimed that he could not go to Cairo because he suffered from seasickness. It was a clear refusal. From that moment on, for Verdi, Mariani was finished. The second choice fell on Maestro Bottesini who was in fashion and whose taste and experience could be relied upon. *Aida's* first night in Cairo lasted from seven o'clock in the evening until half past three in the morning. The khedive himself, with his court, remained in the theater until the end and then sent Verdi a personal telegram of the warmest congratulations. A strange and colorful audience attended the performance, from Copts to Jews, and veiled ladies of the harem, sheltered in three boxes. The success was enormous. But the true premiere of *Aida*, one could say, took place at La Scala on February 8, 1872, conducted by Franco Faccio. Stolz was Aida and Maria Waldmann, the platonic love of Verdi's last years, was Amneris. Verdi attended all the rehearsals, again changing the disposition of the orchestra while, on stage, a band of natives played and three hundred Arab extras and trumpeters participated in the action. At the triumphant end the author was called thirty-two times to the stage. In March 1873, taking advantage of his enforced idleness due to the postponemant of *Aida* in Naples because of Stolz's illness, Verdi composed the *Quartet for strings*.

FOR MANZONI VERDI FELT AUTHENTIC VENERATION

An admirer of Alessandro Manzoni, Verdi, as a young man, had set to music the verses of *Conte di Carmagnola* and *Cinque Maggio*, compositions that were destroyed together with his juvenilia. But with the passing of years, Verdi's admiration for Manzoni became authentic veneration. Both in Turin, one a deputy, the other a senator, they nevertheless did not have occasion to meet because Verdi dared not approach him and the writer, in turn, being very discreet by nature, did not wish to impose on the composer whom he knew to be the enemy of conventionalities. When, later on, a common friend, Countess Maffei, arranged for Verdi to receive a portrait of Manzoni dedicated to him, the maestro was as flustered as a child, blushed and began to perspire. Manzoni's official invitation was delivered a year later in 1868 to Sant'Agata by Clara Maffei whom the Verdis had not seen for quite some time. The meeting took place on June 30th at Manzoni's home and was affectionate and friendly. Verdi reported it to Maffei: "How to explain the very tender, indefinable, new sensation produced in me in the presence of that saint, as you call him? I would have gone down on my knees in front of him if one worshipped men!" When Manzoni died after a fall on coming out of San Fedele's church in Milan, Verdi poured his regret into an intimate, profound, deeply felt composition, the *Messa da requiem*. Because of its excellent acoustics, the church of San Marco in Milan was chosen for its execution and on May 23, 1874, a year after Manzoni's death, the *Requiem* was performed for the first time, conducted by Verdi himself, the soloists being Stolz, Waldmann, Capponi, Maini, with an orchestra of one hundred musicians and one hundred twenty singers in the chorus. People came from all over Europe to hear the *Requiem*. So after the first performance in the sacred silence of the church, the repeat performances took place at La Scala, one more conducted by Verdi, the others by Franco Faccio. The singers appeared in evening clothes and the audience was free to express its enthusiasm, calling out the author's name. The *Requiem* conquered all of Italy: in Bologna it was performed with four pianos, in Ferrara by a band, a fact that made Verdi hit the ceiling. Then it moved through Europe: in London an incredible chorus of 1,200 voices was brought together and the critics wrote that this was the most beautiful religious music since Mozart's *Requiem*.

Below: a famous portrait of Verdi by Boldini; and a drawing showing the maestro conducting the Requiem *at La Scala. Opposite page: the church of San Marco where the first execution of the* Requiem *took place (painting by Luigi Bisi).* Verdi's Requiem *is often criticised for expressing earthly feelings and of not following a liturgical line, but its value consists exactly in its weeping and suffering in the language common to man. Some believe that the "libera me domine" of this monumental* Requiem *had been composed by Verdi for the never completed Mass in memory of Rossini.*

Left: Manzoni at the time he met Verdi. The maestro had first read I promessi sposi *(The Betrothed) when he was sixteen and had re-read it innumerable times. Verdi did not attend Manzoni's funeral, but ten days later he went to Milan to stand in silence before the great man's grave. The drawing below shows what a huge crowd attended the* Requiem *in the church of San Marco, paying homage to Manzoni.*

65

THE DECISIVE MEETING WITH BOITO

In 1860, at Rossini's house in Paris, Verdi met with a young intellectual, Arrigo Boito. And when the matter came up of setting to music a cantata for the International Exposition in London, Verdi gladly accepted the verses written by the young man: *The Hymn of the Nations* bore, for the first time together, the names of Verdi and Boito. But subsequently the latter showed little respect for Verdi; in a poem he went so far as to describe Italian music as "An altar soiled like the walls of a brothel". Verdi took this in bad part and wrote to Ricordi: "If I too, among others, have soiled the altar, let Boito clean it and I will be the first to come and light a candle on it". The resentment lasted and Boito's translations of *Rienzi* and *Tristan und Isolde* certainly did nothing to reduce it. Wagner even wrote Boito a letter of praise, which he published.

But after 1870, Boito's opinion of Verdi changed radically. He liked *Aida* and the *Requiem* immensely. During those years, Tito Ricordi, with great diplomacy, kept Verdi informed of Boito's changes of heart (after its initial failure, his *Mefistofele* had become a triumphant success) and assured the maestro that Boito would consider it a great honor to write a libretto for him. One evening, at dinner, the conversation between Verdi, Ricordi and Maestro Faccio turned to Shakespeare, the scenic possibilities of a libretto based on *Otello*, and Arrigo Boito's name popped up. Verdi showed himself amenable. A few days later Faccio took Boito to see the composer. The real meeting between the two took place at that moment and it opened the way to a fruitful old age for the maestro. Boito, a man of his time, will stimulate in Verdi the process of self-criticism, make him the gift of culture, give him the awareness of every movement of the soul, of every idea, and thus in Verdi will arise modern interests, new inspirations. Arrigo Boito was born in Padua in 1842 (the same year as *Nabucco*) and after his father, a miniaturist painter, abandoned the family he moved to Milan with his mother and was accepted by the conservatory. He travelled in Europe and then, together with his brother Camillo, devoted himself to literature as a member of the "scapigliatura lombarda" movement. As a musician and an intellectual, he proposed a reform of opera, setting an example with his own *Mefistofele* and working until his death on *Nerone*, which was presented posthumously at La Scala in 1924. Besides those he wrote for Verdi, Boito wrote librettos also for Faccio, Ponchielli, Catalani, and Mancinelli.

Maestro Giuseppe Verdi, se

Rocco De Zerbi
"eputato del 5° collegio di Nap

Opposite page: the "Illustrazione Italiana" magazine issues for Otello *and* Falstaff. *Center, from top: opening of the porticoes on Piazza del Duomo in Milan, in the presence of Crown Prince Umberto. At Sant'Agata, with two friends; portrait of Tito Ricordi; page from "Illustrazione Italiana" with photographs of the new senators.*

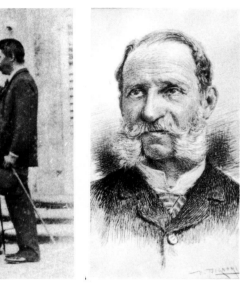

CARLO PRINETTI, senatore. Conte PIER LUIGI BEMBO, sen

Maggiore NICOLA MARSELLI deputato di Pescina Barone FILIPPO deputato di Chiar

On this page: three pictures of Verdi and Boito: taking a walk in Milan; during the rehearsals of Otello; *in the courtyard at Sant'Agata. The* Hymn of the Nations, *important today only because it brought Verdi's and Boito's names together for the first time, was conducted in London on May 24, 1862 by Maestro Luigi Arditi, the author of a famous song:* The Kiss. *The cantata was entitled* Hymn of all Nations *but in it only England, France and Italy were mentioned. Boito's verses ended with an invocation to unified Italy. Arrigo Boito enjoyed great esteem during his life: he obtained the honorary directorship of the Conservatory of Parma, the degree "honoris causa" from the University of Cambridge in 1893, an honor bestowed only on great musicians and the nomination to senator of the Kingdom. He died in Milan on June 10, 1918.*

THE CROWD GOES WILD FOR OTELLO AND FALSTAFF

By the end of 1879 Verdi had already decided to set *Otello* to music but it took a few years to finish: in December, 1855, in fact, he wrote to the French baritone Maurel: "*Otello* is not completely finished, but it is progressing well toward its end". Several singers then wrote to the maestro for parts, but Verdi discouraged everyone, except for Maurel, Tamagno, and the soprano Romilda Pantaleoni. *Otello* was completed on November 1, 1866; the premiere at La Scala was set for February 15, 1887. Verdi was 74 years old and, most wisely, being concerned about his age, he reserved the right to withdraw the opera at any moment during rehearsal. But everything went well. Expectations were frenetic: fifteen minutes before the curtain, the theater was packed and the adjacent streets remained crowded during the entire performance. On the podium was Franco Faccio. Already after the first act, the author was called to the stage amid great applause and at the end when he reappeared a simultaneous shout of enthusiasm rose to greet him and he bent his head, smiling through his tears. When Verdi left La Scala that night the crowd unhitched his horses and pulled the carriage all the way to the Hotel Milano, where the maesto habitually stayed, and then they insisted that Tamagno, from the hotel's balcony, repeat the "Esultate" aria from *Otello*. As he retired that evening, Verdi said to his friends: "If I were thirty years younger, tomorrow I would begin a new opera, but on the condition that Boito be my librettist". This new opera will be written, and it will be called *Falstaff*. The first hint can be found in a letter that Verdi wrote to Boito from Montecatini: "And what if I could not sustain the effort? If I should not be able to finish the music?" The announcement that the opera was in the making came during a diner at Ricordi's house. Boito stood up to toast "Fatbelly", but nobody understood because all those present were slim. Only when Boito said: "I drink to the health of Falstaff!" did they understand that he was referring to a new opera. But when will it be performed? Verdi is old and works only a few hours a day, when he feels like it. It will be said that *Falstaff* is the vacation of his old age.

Falstaff was presented at La Scala on February 9, 1893, when Verdi was almost eighty years old. Maestro Mascheroni conducted; this time too, and for the last time, the success was tremendous, and the grand old man was able to escape from the crowd's enthusiasm only by slipping out through a side door.

Below: a scene from Otello *and the first interpreters of the opera: tenor Tamagno, soprano Panataleoni, and baritone Maurel, who went to Sant'Agata to study their parts with Verdi. The costumes were taken from the Venetian picture galleries, while the sets were by Carlo Ferrario. Also for* Falstaff *the sets will be researched in old English houses. To attend the performances of* Otello *at La Scala, important personalities arrived from all over Europe. The event was looked forward to with great interest both in Italy and abroad. Also on that occasion the prices of tickets were astronomical and the scalpers made a fortune.*

Left: two drawings showing the opening night of Otello at the Opéra and the president of the French Republic introducing Verdi to the audience at the Opéra during the applause for Falstaff. Directly below: an illustration of Falstaff preserved at the La Scala Theatrical Museum in Milan. For Falstaff, King Umberto sent Verdi a telegram and cordially received him at the Quirinale Palace for the opera's Roman premiere. Photograph in center: Verdi with tenor Tamagno. Bottom: the premiere of Falstaff at La Scala. On the score of his last labor, Verdi had written Falstaff's words: "It's all over, go, go, old John, go your way".

Below: a bust of Giuseppina when quite old, by the sculptor Vincenzo Gemito. In 1887, in Naples, a young man, ill-fed and dressed in rags, had broken through the protective circle surrounding Verdi, and told the maestro that he was a poor sculptor named Vincenzo Gemito. In his ardent eyes Verdi had recognized the flame of art and had immediately helped him, even paying the exoneration fee to keep the young man from being called up by the army, so that he could remain in Naples to work and help support his indigent family. Out of gratitude, Gemito portrayed, with inspired élan, the features of the maestro and of Giuseppina at the hotel in Naples.

STREPPONI WAS A GIFT OF PROVIDENCE FOR THE MAESTRO

Opposite page, above the assassination of King Umberto I at Monza in a sketch by Gennaro Amato. Verdi, almost ninety years old, was very much perturbed by the tragic event and was tempted to set to music a prayer written for the occasion by Queen Margherita. But he only put down a few notes and they were his last.

Further below: two old photographs of Verdi at Montecatini. He is sitting at a table with some of his closest friends and the unforgettable Stolz. Directly below, in Milan: the rest home to which Verdi willed the royalties to all his operas performed in Italy and abroad.

For years Verdi had been thinking of erecting in Milan a rest home for musicians and, in 1895, he entrusted the project to the architect Camillo Boito, Arrigo's brother. As was his habit, Verdi took an interest in even the smallest details of the undertaking and in May, 1896, he deposited the funds necessary for the entire project. He intended that those who had devoted their lives to music should have a decorous roof over their heads, and to the Casa di Riposo, which to this day welcomes in Milan hundreds of old singers and musician, he left in his will all the royalties to his operas.

On November 14, 1897, after several years of ill health, Giuseppina Strepponi died of pneumonia at Sant'Agata. The loss was severe, but the maestro bore it with dignity. He kissed Giuseppina for the last time, then he sent for a friend, the lawyer Amilcare Martinelli. He received him standing up, next to a table covered with documents, his head lowered, his cheeks flushed with emotion and did not say a word. Giuseppina was buried in the Monumentale cemetery in Milan where Verdi had bought two plots. As a singer, Giuseppina Strepponi had shared with him the triumph of *Nabucco*, and as his wife, she had accompanied him all the way to *Falstaff*, following him, loving him, always advising him for the best, watching over him without ever being importunate. Like Barezzi, like Merelli, Strepponi had also been a gift of providence in Verdi's life. In her will she wrote these concluding words: "And now farewell, my Verdi. As we were united in life, may God unite our hearts in paradise."

After Giuseppina's death, the composer's physical decline began: his heart was in disorder, his hands were afflicted by a continuous tremor. To escape the anguish of his memories both in Genoa and at Sant'Agata, he decided to move to Milan. Before Giuseppina's passing, he had written a *Te Deum* and *Pezzi Sacri*, thus his last music bore the clear mark of someone whose thought has turned to God. *Te Deum* and *Pezzi Sacri* were performed in Paris during Holy Week in 1898, then at Turin, under the baton of a young maestro who had met Verdi and was beginning to be appreciated as a scrupulous interpreter of his works, Arturo Toscanini.

300,000 PEOPLE FILLED THE STREETS AND TOSCANINI DIRECTED THE CHORUS DURING THE FUNERAL

The shadows were beginning to descend on Sant'Agata where Verdi had returned to spend the summer, looked after with devotion by Maria Carrara. His legs were unsteady, his hearing had deteriorated, he always wore black and when he approached the piano it was only to play the dramatic motif from *Don Carlos*, "Dormirò sol nel mio manto regal..." (I shall sleep alone in my regal mantle). As the months went by he grew more feeble, it became necessary to carry him out into the garden on a wheel chair. In December, 1900, always attended by Maria Carrara, he was moved to Milan and settled in a large room of

Hotel Milano, his favorite hotel. There he spent a pleasant Christmas with his dearest friends, Teresa Stolz, Boito, Pascarella, and the Ricordi family. The grand old man crossed the threshold of the new century. On January 21, 1901, as the maid was helping him dress, he fell into her arms, struck by apoplexy, and did not recover consciousness. It is said that during his last moments he smiled at the priest who came to administer extreme unction at dawn on January 24th.

Telegrams with messages of hope arrived from everywhere, while a silent crowd stood waiting for news in the street which

72

was covered with straw to muffle the noise made by the carriages. The playwright Giuseppe Giacosa bowed, crushed, at Verdi's bedside, reported that the maestro was serene and looked as if he were asleep. The expected death came on January 27, at ten minutes to three in the morning. In keeping with the precise instructions found in his will, Giuseppe Verdi was buried with the greatest simplicity on January 30, at dawn, with two priests, two candles, one cross, in the Cimitero Monumentale. But when, a month later, the authorization arrived from Town Hall for the burial in his Casa Di Riposo, the removal of the body offered the opportunity for the most extraordinary and moving expression of affection by the Milanese. More than three hundred thousand people crowded the streets, filled the balconies, or perched on trees. The magnificent hearse, designed by two architects, was followed by hundreds of wreaths, while an immense chorus conducted by Arturo Toscanini sang for the maestro the moving notes of his young glory: "Va, pensiero, sull'ali dorate..."

Ten years later, on the centenary of his birth, all his most important operas were performed at La Scala.

Even when advancing in a procession Verdi's characters all have a well-defined physiognomy. They rest on a number of fundamental concepts: God, the nation, the people, justice, and liberty. After the first operas in which it was the mass, as in Nabucco or I Lombardi, gradually the individual will come to the fore, with the noblest sentiments and the most dramatic passions. The character of the father, above all, was given masterful depth by Verdi in Rigoletto, Germont, Simon Boccanegra, and Amonasro. Verdi has sung, wept and cursed through these characters of his. Having, with the passing of the years, become old and wise, with ironic and mocking Falstaff he decided to leave us a message for the serene acceptance of life. Few other characters are as popular throughout the world as the protagonists of Verdi's operas, whom we see here, gathered around the maestro in a drawing by Edoardo Matania.

Verdi is the last monumental figure in Italian opera; with him the cycle started three centuries earlier with Monteverdi comes to a close. "Verdi's advent changed the musical panorama of the 19th century," wrote Fedele d'Amico, "because very early on Verdi stopped creating simple inventive material arranged summarily, a repertory of musical and dramatic situations and sentiments left to stand on their own merits, to which only a great singer could impart form." Alberto Savinio sets down for *Otello*, in particular, a definition valid for all of Verdi's art: "It is a music that Michelangelo, blind, would have recognized by touch." And Stravinsky summed up Verdi when he wrote: "I claim that there is more substance and real invention in the aria 'La donna è mobile', than in the rhetoric and vociferations of the entire Wagnerian tetralogy." Verdi was a genius of Shakespearian stature. He sang the emotions of man, he wept their tears, he was able to embody in music everybody's joys and sorrows. He did so by delving deeply into his characters, by developing techniques and conceptions which traced from *Oberto* to *Falstaff* an arc of progression and perfection almost impossible to find in the development of any other opera composer.

1813 · October 10: Giuseppe Verdi is born at Le Roncole, town of Busseto, in a poor family: his father Carlo, a storekeeper, his mother Luigia, a spinner. The same year, in Leipzing, the birth of Richard Wagner.

1827 · The death of Ludwig van Beethoven in Vienna.

1828 · A performance of the *Barber of Seville*, at the Busseto theater. An opening symphony composed by Verdi is substituted for Rossini's overture. It is the first work by the very young (fifteen year old) composer to be performed in public.

1828-32 · Writes several sacred pieces, marches for the village band, and vocal and orchestral compositions.

1832 · Goes to Milan to attend the Conservatory but is not accepted. However, Maestro Lavigna takes him as a pupil.

1835 · The thirty-five year old Vincenzo Bellini dies in Paris.

1836 · Verdi marries Margherita Barezzi, the daughter of his benefactor.

1839 · In Milan he meets the impresario Merelli and the singer Giuseppina Strepponi. November: successful opening at La Scala of *Oberto*.

1840 · Death of his wife, shortly after the death of his two small children.

1842 · March 9, triumph of *Nabucco* at La Scala. The opera was commissioned by Merelli, who thus lifted him out of the depression caused by the family tragedies that had befallen him. Arrigo Boito is born in Padua.

1843-51 · Writes and produces thirteen operas, among them: *I Lombardi alla prima crociata, I due Foscari* and *Macbeth*. The librettos are by Solera, Piave, Cammarano, and Maffei; the operas are performed in Milan, Rome, Naples, Venice, Trieste and London.

1844 · Verdi acquires in Busseto the estate of Sant'Agata, which from then on becomes his refuge and the place where his masterpieces are born.

1847 · The ties of affection between Verdi and the singer Strepponi become closer.

1848 · March 18, to 22: Milan's Five Days. Gaetano Donizetti dies.

1849 · This is the year when so many hopes of the Italian patriots collapse: defeat at Novara and the abdication of Carlo Alberto, failure of the Ten Days in Brescia, fall of the Roman Republic, the surrender of Venice.

1851 · Verdi's mother dies.

1851-62 · He composes *Rigoletto, Il Trovatore, La Traviata, I Vespri Siciliani* (premiere in Paris), *Simon Boccanegra, Un ballo in maschera, La forza del destino* (staged in St. Petersburg).

1859 · Verdi marries Giuseppina Strepponi. Meanwhile, the events of the Risorgimento make him especially responsive to the nation's needs. He would like to take up arms but cannot for reasons of health; however, he comes to the aid of the wounded and the families of those who died in the war. September: he is sent to Turin to present Vittorio Emanuele II with the vote of annexation of the people of Parma.

1861 · Proclamation of the Kingdom of Italy. Verdi agrees, on Cavour's insistence, to present his candidacy for deputy in the first Italian parliament and is elected for the Liberal Party. June 6,: death of Camillo Benso di Cavour.

1863-71 · These years see the birth only of *Don Carlos* (staged for the first time in Paris in 1867), but mark a period of absorption and meditation during which he revises and reworks some of his operas.

1867 · In this year Verdi loses his father, his benefactor Barezzi and his friends Piave.

1868 · Gioacchino Rossini dies at Passy near Paris.

1871 · Triumph at Cairo of *Aida* (Ghislanzoni's libretto).

1873 · *Quartet for strings*.

1874 · First execution in Milan of the *Requiem Mass* in memory of Alessandro Manzoni, who had died the year before.

1875 · Verdi is named senator for life.

1879 · Impresario Merelli dies in Milan.

1880 · *Pater noster* and *Ave Maria*.

1881 · Reworks *Simon Boccanegra* with libretto revised by Arrigo Boito.

1883 · Richard Wagner dies in Venice.

1887 · Between the performance of *Aida* (1871) and that of *Otello* (1887) stretches a long period of study and meditation which results in Verdi's masterpiece composed for a libretto by Boito, who had become his faithful and devoted collaborator.

1888 · Death of the publisher Tito Ricordi; his place is taken by his son, Giulio.

1893 · *Falstaff* is presented in Milan.

1897 · Verdi's second wife, Giuseppina Strepponi, dies.

1898 · In Paris the *Pezzi Sacri* (*Te Deum, Laudi alla Vergine, Stabat*) are performed.

1901 · January 27: Verdi's death in Milan. His mortal remains are later removed to the chapel of the Rest Home for Musicians which he had founded.